Everyman's Poetry

Everyman, I will go with thee,
and be thy guide

John Milton

Selected and edited by GORDON CAMPBELL

University of Leicester

EVERYMAN
J. M. Dent · London

J. M. Dent
Orion Publishing Group
Orion House
5 Upper St Martin's Lane
London WC2H 9EA

Typeset by Deltatype Ltd, Ellesmere Port, Cheshire
Printed in Great Britain by
The Guernsey Press Co. Ltd, Guernsey, C.I.

British Library Cataloguing-in-Publication
Data is available upon request.

ISBN 0 460 87813 1

Contents

Note on the Author and Editor

JOHN MILTON (1608–74) was born in London, the son of a scrivener. He was educated at St Paul's School and Christ's College, Cambridge. On leaving Cambridge Milton returned to his parents' house in Hammersmith, and in about 1635 the family moved to Horton, in Buckinghamshire; during these years Milton undertook a vigorous programme of private study. In 1638 and 1639 he travelled in Italy, and when he returned to England became a school teacher in his own home. In 1649 Milton was appointed Secretary for Foreign Tongues to the Council of State. He was already blind in one eye, and in 1652 he lost the sight of his other eye. After the restoration of Charles II in 1660 Milton retired to private life.

In 1634 Milton received a commission to write a masque for the Earl of Bridgewater; the masque, which is now known as *Comus*, is Milton's first important work to deal with the theme of temptation, which was to be the central theme of his epics. In 1637 Milton composed 'Lycidas', a pastoral elegy which commemorates a fellow student at Cambridge. During the Commonwealth and Protectorate Milton wrote a large number of prose works, and also composed his sonnets. Blindness and enforced retirement gave him the leisure to write *Paradise Lost* and *Samson Agonistes*.

GORDON CAMPBELL is Professor of Renaissance Literature at the University of Leicester and President of the English Association. He has written widely on English Renaissance literature, especially on John Milton, and has recently completed a documentary chronology of Milton. He is editor of the interdisciplinary journal *Renaissance Studies*.

Chronology of Milton's Life

Year	Age	Life
1608		Born 9 December in Bread Street, London
1615	6	(?) Enters St Paul's School
1618	9	Portrait painted, possibly by Cornelius Janssen
1624	15	Translations of Psalms CXIV and CXXXVI
1625	16	Admitted to Christ's College, Cambridge (12 February)
1626	17	(?) 'On the Death of a Fair Infant'
1628	19	'At a Vacation Exercise'
1629	20	Takes B.A., 16 March; 'Nativity Ode', 25 December
1630	21	'The Passion', 26–28 March; 'On Shakespeare'
1631	22	'Marchioness of Winchester'; 'University Carrier'; Sonnet XVII
1632	23	Takes M.A., 3 July; moves home to Hammersmith

Chronology of his Times

Year	Cultural Context	Historical Events
1608	*Coriolanus* performed	Champlain founds Quebec
1609	Shakespeare, *Sonnets*	Tokugawa shogunate (–1867)
1610	Jonson, *Alchemist* performed	
1611	King James Bible *Tempest* performed	Bermudas settled
1612	Webster, *White Devil* performed	
1614	Jonson, *Bartholomew Fair* performed	Addled Parliament
1616	Jonson, folio *Works*	Death of Shakespeare
1617		Pocahontas at Court
1618		Thirty Years War (–1648)
1619		Dutch found Batavia
1620		*Mayflower* lands
1622		Virginia settlers massacred
1623	Shakespeare, 'First Folio'	
1625		Charles I crowned
1626	Bacon, *New Atlantis*	
1627		Anglo-French War
1628	Harvey, 'Circulation of the Blood'	
1629		Charles I dissolves parliament (–1640)
1632	Shakespeare, 'Second Folio'	

Year	Age	Life
1633	24	(?) 'The Circumcision'
1634	25	*Comus* performed, 29 September; Psalm CXIV (Greek version)
1635	26	(?) Moves to Horton
1637	28	Mother (Sara) dies, 3 April; *Comus* published; 'Lycidas' composed (November)
1638	29	'Lycidas' published; Milton leaves for Italy (April?)
1639	30	Returns to England (July?)
1640	31	Moves to Aldersgate
1642	33	Marries Mary Powell (July?); Sonnet VIII
1643	34	Parliament issues Licensing Order, 14 June
1644	35	*Of Education* (June); *Areopagitica* (November)
1645	36	Sonnets XI and XII
1646	37	*Poems* published (2 January?), dated 1645; Sonnets XIII and XIV; 'On the New Forcers'; daughter Anne born, 29 July
1647	38	Father (John) dies; Milton moves to High Holborn
1648	39	Psalms LXXX–LXXXVIII (April); Sonnet XV; daughter Mary born, 25 October
1649	40	Appointed Secretary for Foreign Tongues, 15 March; moves to Scotland Yard
1651	42	Son John born, 16 March; moves to Petty France; eyesight failing
1652	43	Onset of complete blindness; birth of daughter Deborah, 2 May; death of wife Mary (5 May?) and son John (June); Sonnets XIX (?), XVI, XVII and (?) XIX
1653	44	Psalms I–VIII
1655	46	Sonnets XVIII, XXI and XXII
1656	47	Marries Katherine Woodcock, 12 November

Year	Cultural Context	Historical Events
1633	Donne, *Poems* Herbert, *The Temple*	Laud becomes archbishop (–1645)
1634	Oberammergau passion play performed	
1636		Harvard College founded
1637	Corneille, *Le Cid* performed	
1639		First Bishops' War
1640	Carew, *Poems*	Second Bishops' War Long Parliament (–1653)
1641		Irish rebellion
1642	Browne, *Religio Medici*	English Civil War (–1649) Tasman lands in New Zealand
1643		Louis XIV crowned (–1715)
1644		Ch'ing dynasty (–1912)
1646	Vaughan, *Poems*	
1647		Execution of Laud
1648		First Fronde (–1649)
1649		Execution of Charles I
1650	Anne Bradstreet, *Tenth Muse*	
1651	Hobbes, *Leviathan*	Second Fronde (–1653)
1652		First Anglo-Dutch War (–1654)
1653	Walton, *Complete Angler*	Taj Mahal completed
1655		English capture Jamaica
1656		Bernini completes St Peter's (Rome) Anglo-Spanish War (–1659)

Year	Age	Life
1657	48	Daughter Katherine born, 19 October
1658	49	Death of wife Katherine, 3 February, and daughter Katherine, 17 March; Sonnet XXIII (?)
1660	51	In hiding and subsequently in custody
1663	54	Marries Elizabeth Minshull, 24 February
1665	56	Moves to Chalfont St Giles to escape plague
1667	58	*Paradise Lost* published in 10 books (August)
1669	60	Moves to Artillery Walk
1671	62	*Paradise Regained* and *Samson Agonistes* published
1672	63	
1673	64	Second edition of *Poems* published
1674	65	Second edition of *Paradise Lost* published in 12 books (July); Milton dies on 8 November (?); buried on 12 November in St Giles Cripplegate

Year	Cultural Context	Historical Events
1658		Death of Cromwell
1660		Restoration of Charles II
1661		English acquire Bombay
1662		Dunkirk sold to France
1664		British capture New Amsterdam
1665		Great Plague
		Second Dutch War (–1667)
1666	Bunyan, *Grace Abounding*	Fire of London
1667	Racine, *Andromaque* performed	
1669	Racine, *Britannicus* performed	
1670	Racine, *Bérénice* performed	Hudson's Bay Company incorporated
1672		Third Dutch War (–1674)
1673		Test Act passed

Introduction

John Milton is the greatest poet of the English Puritan tradition. The difficulty, of course, is that modern readers find the term 'Puritan' slightly off-putting. The automobile manufacturer that produces a model called the Cavalier does so in the belief that the term is suggestive of poise and grace and stylishness; there is no model called the Puritan, because the association with austerity and a pleasure-denying mentality would not sell cars. The popular image of the seventeenth-century Puritan is, like most stereotypes, somewhat less than a half-truth. Puritans were not so much opposed to cakes and ale as they were in favour of honest government that reflected the wishes of the people rather than the interests of an hereditary ruling class. In that sense Milton became a Puritan, and during the years of Cromwell's Commonwealth and Protectorate he worked for the government and defended Parliament's decision to execute the king and establish a republic. When Milton was a young man in the late 1620s and 1630s, however, the term Puritan is not so useful, because the country had not yet divided into rival supporters of king and parliament. In that period Milton could better be described as a young man who wanted to become a great poet.

The companion poems 'L'Allegro' and 'Il Penseroso' must be counted among the finest poems of Milton's youth. Companion poems were popular in the late sixteenth and early seventeenth centuries. It should be remembered that the second poem in the pair was not always written at the same time, or even by the same person, as the first poem. Marlowe's 'Passionate Shepherd to his Love', for example, was written as an autonomous poem, and later Ralegh wrote a companion poem, 'The Nymph's Reply to the Shepherd'. Marlowe's poem concludes with the couplet

> If these delights thy mind may move,
> Then live with me and be my love.

and Ralegh's with a similar couplet. These invitations are clearly the originals of the couplets which conclude Milton's poems.

'L'Allegro', or a portion of it, may have been written as an independent poem. If, however, 'Il Penseroso' does represent a later stage in Milton's poetic development, then it would seem fitting to view the thought in the poems as progressing from 'L'Allegro' to 'Il Penseroso' rather than to see the points of view as two carefully-balanced alternatives. There are many exact parallels between the poems: the metre of 'Il Penseroso' imitates that of 'L'Allegro', the preludes are similar, and the catalogues of pleasures contain many exact oppositions. On the other hand there are some indications that 'Il Penseroso' has the upper hand. In the ten-line preludes to the poems, for example, one notes that whilst the deluding joys banished by 'Il Penseroso' bear some resemblance to the joys celebrated in 'L'Allegro', the melancholy banished by 'L'Allegro' is of a different kind from that celebrated by 'Il Penseroso'. A similar weighting of the scales in favour of 'Il Penseroso' is evident in the final movements of the poems, for not only is 'Il Penseroso' longer, but it also concludes with a religious experience that has no parallel in the earlier poem.

A Masque Presented at Ludlow Castle, which since the late seventeenth century has been known as *Comus*, was performed before the Earl of Bridgewater and his guests on 29 September 1634. Although both Milton and Lawes termed *Comus* a masque, it is not a representative Stuart masque, as a comparison with Jonson's masques or the masques incorporated in Shakespeare's plays makes readily apparent. *Comus* is not alone among masques in absorbing into its fabric elements from related forms such as the moral interlude and the pastoral play, but the dominance of dramatic dialogue over the music and spectacle is unusual in a play that retains so many of the traditional features of the masque. The journey to Ludlow in *Comus* reflects the processional element in traditional masques. The element of compliment in court masques is presented indirectly in *Comus* through a portrayal of the virtue of Lord Bridgewater's children, who at the dramatic climax of the masque are presented to the Earl and Countess as 'three fair branches of your own'; the virtue of the children is a compliment to their parents.

The subject of *Comus* is virtue. As virtue in women was thought to manifest itself in chastity, which for an unmarried woman meant virginity, and as the central character in the play is the Lady, Milton's exposition of virtue is couched in terms of chastity and virginity. While Comus is on the stage virtue is tested; this portion of the play constitutes Milton's first dramatic exposition of the theme of temptation, a theme to which he was to return in *Paradise Lost* and *Samson Agonistes*. When Comus is replaced by Sabrina – the parts may have been played by the same actor – chastity is celebrated rather than tested, and becomes a positive virtue rather than an inhibiting one. The dramatic realization of this aspect of virtue is reserved until the end of the masque, but Milton had allowed the Lady to articulate the positive aspect of chastity in her first speech:

> O welcome pure-eyed Faith, white-handed Hope,
> Thou hovering angel girt with golden wings,
> And thou unblemished form of Chastity!

The mention of faith and hope in line 213 naturally leads Milton's readers or listeners to expect a description of charity. Milton skilfully prolongs the expectation by spending his next line on a visual image of hope, and at the end of line 215 suddenly fulfils the anticipation of charity with a presentation of chastity. The effect of this paranomasia is an alteration in the meaning of chastity. The word normally carries the suggestion of a withholding or suppressing of natural desires in the interests of a lofty ideal, and later in the poem Comus exploits this negative idea of chastity. The Lady's speech anticipates these arguments by forcefully conjoining charity and chastity, and so removes the stigma of withholding from chastity, which becomes an image of love. The Lady has transformed chastity into a positive virtue which represents the giving of love rather than its denial.

The greatest of Milton's minor poems is 'Lycidas', which is justly regarded as one of the finest poems in the English language. 'Lycidas' was first published in a collection of poems commemorating the death of Edward King, a Fellow of Christ's College. Milton had probably not known King well, but was none the less deeply moved by his premature death. Milton's poem originated in a desire to lament this specific death, but in the act of composition Milton transcended his ostensible subject to produce a meditation on personal mortality that retains the power to move readers centuries after King and his mourners have turned to dust.

'Lycidas' is a pastoral elegy, which was a popular form in the late Middle Ages and the Renaissance; in the nineteenth century the pastoral elegy was chosen by Shelley for 'Adonais' and by Arnold for 'Thyrsis', their laments for Keats and Clough.

In pastoral elegy the poet and his subject are described as shepherds or goatherds. As the form evolved it became increasingly distanced from shepherd life in ancient Sicily. Virgil elevated the style of pastoral elegy and included in it personal and public comments unrelated to the death of the person represented as a shepherd. Christian writers of the late Middle Ages and the Renaissance seized on the joyous conclusion of Virgil's Eclogue V as a model for the Christian consolation at the end of their elegies. In the Renaissance pastoral these innovations were combined with traditional features such as the procession of mourners and the lament of nature, and with features that had appeared in other pastoral poems, such as the ecclesiastical satire in the eclogues of Petrarch (VI and VII). The pastoral elegy was established in England by Spenser in the November eclogue of the *Shepherd's Calendar* and 'Astrophel', his lament for Sidney. 'Lycidas' is firmly rooted in the tradition of pastoral elegy and displays many of its characteristic features. Milton was not bound by the tradition – he omitted, for example, the refrain which was a prominent feature of ancient pastoral elegies – but drew on it to shape and temper his emotions and poetical impulses.

The composition of a lament for Edward King prompted Milton to reflect on the meaning and purpose of human life. King was a young man who had shared with Milton the experience of the same tutor in the same college, who had shared Milton's commitment to the Protestant faith, and who, like Milton, had published a few poems. King's premature death called into question Milton's ambition to become a great Christian poet:

> Alas! What boots it with uncessant care
> To tend the homely slighted shepherd's trade,
> And strictly meditate the thankless muse?

'Lycidas' is a quest for an answer to that question. At the beginning of the poem Milton's imagination is constrained by the thought of his own death:

> So may some gentle muse
> With lucky words favour my destined urn,
> And as he passes turn,
> And bid fair peace be to my sable shroud.

At this moment the poem is saved from what seems an inevitable plunge into self-pity by the impersonality of the pastoral mode. Milton gradually transcends not only the death of King but also the brutal reminder of his own mortality that King's death afforded. At its most profound level the poem considers the purpose of human existence and effort in a world in which evil is allowed to flourish and virtuous men like King are allowed to die. Milton's characteristic integrity of mind prevents him from accepting the platitudinous assurances of Phoebus, and from acquiescing in the consolation offered by the ceremony of throwing poetical flowers on the hearse of Lycidas. Consolation finally comes with the realization that Lycidas 'is not dead', for he is experiencing the inexpressible joy of heaven and, as the 'genius of the shore', is continuing to minister to mankind as he did on earth. Milton's calm of mind is restored, and his detachment from his grief is marked by a change of poetic voice in the last stanza of the poem. Milton is reconciled to mortality, and has summoned up the strength to enter 'fresh woods, and pastures new'.

In 1649 Milton was appointed Secretary for Foreign Tongues to the Council of State, and his formidable abilities as a pamphleteer were turned to the defence of the Commonwealth, and in particular to the defence of the execution of Charles I. Milton continued to defend his republican principles until the eve of the Restoration in 1660. During these two decades of pamphleteering Milton continually reminded his readers of his plans to write a national epic. But his only finished English poems composed during this period are his sonnets.

Milton's sonnets constitute an important contribution to the English sonnet tradition. Sometimes his subject so inflamed his imagination that his sonnets achieved greatness. In Sonnet XVIII his horror at the barbarity of the recent massacre in Piedmont is condensed into an explosive sonnet; in Sonnet XIX, on the other hand, quiet reflection on his blindness has impelled him to write a sonnet that begins in despair and frustration and rises to a sense of spiritual calmness that recalls the ending of 'Lycidas'.

Milton's English predecessors in the art of the sonnet had developed conventions that had originated in Petrarch's sonnets and then been modified by poets adapting the form to their own purposes. Shakespeare, for example, turned the Petrarchan sestet into a third quatrain and an independently rhymed couplet. Milton continued this tradition of innovation, but experimented with one eye on Italian poets (particularly Giovanni Della Casa) who had attempted similar variations. Like these Italian poets, Milton sometimes chose to blur the distinction between octave and sestet by making both sense and syntax continuous between the eighth and ninth lines. The fluidity and continuity of thought which Milton is able to achieve by allowing his sentences to come to a natural conclusion remind one of the style of Shakespeare's last plays, in which the sense flows from line to line with scarcely any end-stopping. Milton's poetry similarly flourished when he over-rode the constraints of form. The exploration of this freedom is an important element in the poetic accomplishment of *Paradise Lost*, in which, as Milton explains in his prefatory note, 'the sense [is] variously drawn out from one verse into another'.

Paradise Lost is the supreme example of the epic in English. His purpose, as he explained at the conclusion of the opening invocation, was 'to justify the ways of God to men' (line 26). This may seem an odd aspiration, because Christians tend to think that the ways of God are inscrutable and do not stand in need of justification. The collapse in 1660 of what Milton and his fellow Puritans saw as God's government on earth in favour of rule by a corrupt and sexually profligate king, however, raised fundamental questions, perhaps for the only time in the history of English Christianity, about the ways of God. The question of how a just God could allow an unjust Restoration to take place is at the moral centre of *Paradise Lost*.

In the first two books of the poem Milton presents Satan, the master of illusory heroism and the self-proclaimed saviour of those angels who followed him into Hell. Satan's speech has a radical edge: when he says of Hell that 'Here at least/ We shall be free' (I 258–9) he sounds like a New England colonist escaping persecu-tion. Similarly, Mammon praises Hell as a place where angels can be 'free, and to none accountable, preferring/ Hard liberty before the easy yoke/ Of servile pomp' (II 255–7). Milton's point is clear: the most effective rebels against God are those who speak the language of radical revolution in order to further their own interests. The godly revolution failed not because Charles II invaded from France with a large army, but rather because, in Milton's view, the revolution was betrayed from within by those who spoke as its supporters. Satan is constructed as an antitype of Jesus, because he represents the figure of the Antichrist: he has twelve disciples, and, because in the minds of seventeenth-century Puritans the Pope was associated with the Antichrist, his palace is modelled on St Peter's Basilica in Rome. Similarly, because the life of Jesus was deemed to conform to the model of heroic tragedy, in that he descended from Heaven in order to die for humankind, so Satan presents himself as a tragic hero. In some ways he resembles villainous tragic heroes such as Macbeth, but there are many indications that the reader is supposed to regard him as a fraud who pretends to equality but sits raised 'above his fellows, with monarchal pride' (II 428).

As a young man Milton had explored the dramatic potential of poetry in *Comus*, and on that occasion he had drawn on the masque convention of the delayed journey to provide a structure for his own masque. When Milton returned to poetic drama to write *Samson Agonistes* (at an unknown date) he again incorporated an interrupted journey into the fabric of his poem, but this time he transformed the outward journey of the masque into an interior journey, Samson's progress towards spiritual regeneration. Milton's dramatic poem is modelled on the tragedies of ancient Greece, which were, in seventeenth-century England, read rather than acted; *Samson Agonistes* was similarly intended to be read, and was never performed during Milton's lifetime. The form of the play is Greek, but the characterization of Samson is contemporary: in his opening soliloquy Samson can be seen to be far more self-conscious that the protagonists of ancient drama, and as such has far more in common with Hamlet than with Oedipus.

The conventions of Greek drama were admirably suited to Milton's purposes. The fate that dominates Greek tragedy becomes for Samson the promise that he will deliver 'Israel from Philistian yoke' (line 39). Greek fate would have been readily translated into Christian providence by Milton's Puritan readers. Those readers would also have shared the common Puritan belief that they had a sacred obligation to search themselves for indications of God's plan for their lives; Samson's cast of mind would not have seemed remote. Similarly, Samson's spiritual solitude was part of the seventeenth-century Puritan experience; just as Bunyan's Christian leaves his family behind as he embarks on his spiritual journey, so Samson is alone. Indeed, Milton's Samson and Bunyan's Christian must seek their salvation in a world in which God does not intervene, because Puritans believed that the age of miracles had ended with the early church. *Samson Agonistes*, like *Paradise Lost*, is on one level an attempt to explore the moral questions raised by the problem of a God who does not intervene to stifle evil.

GORDON CAMPBELL

John Milton

On Time

Fly, envious Time, till thou run out thy race;
Call on the lazy leaden-stepping Hours,
Whose speed is but the heavy plummet's pace;
And glut thyself with what thy womb devours,
Which is no more than what is false and vain,   5
And merely mortal dross;
So little is our loss,
So little is thy gain.
For, when as each thing bad thou hast entombed,
And, last of all, thy greedy self consumed,   10
Then long Eternity shall greet our bliss
With an individual kiss,
And joy shall overtake us as a flood;
When every thing that is sincerely good,
And perfectly divine,   15
With Truth, and Peace, and Love, shall ever shine
About the supreme throne
Of him, to whose happy-making sight alone
When once our heavenly-guided soul shall climb,
Then, all this earthly grossness quit,   20
Attired with stars we shall for ever sit,
    Triumphing over Death, and Chance, and thee, O Time!

At a Solemn Music

Blest pair of sirens, pledges of heaven's joy,
Sphere-born harmonious sisters, Voice and Verse,
Wed your divine sounds, and mixed power employ,
Dead things with inbreathed sense able to pierce,
And to our high-raised fantasy present   5
That undisturbèd song of pure concent,
Aye sung before the sapphire-coloured throne

To him that sits thereon,
With saintly shout and solemn jubilee;
Where the bright seraphim in burning row   10
Their loud uplifted angel-trumpets blow,
And the cherubic host in thousand choirs
Touch their immortal harps of golden wires,
With those just spirits that wear victorious palms,
Hymns devout and holy psalms   15
Singing everlastingly;
That we on earth, with undiscording voice,
May rightly answer that melodious noise;
As once we did, till disproportioned sin
Jarred against nature's chime, and with harsh din   20
Broke the fair music that all creatures made
To their great Lord, whose love their motion swayed
In perfect diapason, whilst they stood
In first obedience, and their state of good.
O may we soon again renew that song,   25
And keep in tune with heaven, till God ere long
To his celestial consort us unite,
To live with him, and sing in endless morn of light.

L'Allegro

Hence, loathed Melancholy,
    Of Cerberus and blackest Midnight born
In Stygian cave forlorn
    'Mongst horrid shapes, and shrieks, and sights unholy;
Find out some uncouth cell,   5
    Where brooding Darkness spreads his jealous wings,
And the night-raven sings;
    There, under ebon shades and low-browed rocks,
As ragged as thy locks,
    In dark Cimmerian desert ever dwell.   10
But come, thou Goddess fair and free,
In heaven yclept Euphrosyne,

And by men, heart-easing Mirth;
Whom lovely Venus, at a birth,
With two sister Graces more, 15
To ivy-crownèd Bacchus bore;
Or whether (as some sager sing)
The frolic wind that breathes the spring,
Zephyr, with Aurora playing,
As he met her once a-Maying, 20
There, on beds of violets blue,
And fresh-blown roses washed in dew,
Filled her with thee, a daughter fair,
So buxom, blithe, and debonair.
Haste thee, Nymph, and bring with thee 25
Jest, and youthful Jollity,
Quips and cranks and wanton wiles,
Nods and becks and wreathèd smiles,
Such as hang on Hebe's cheek,
And love to live in dimple sleek; 30
Sport that wrinkled Care derides,
And Laughter holding both his sides.
Come, and trip it, as you go,
On the light fantastic toe;
And in thy right hand lead with thee 35
The mountain-nymph, sweet Liberty;
And, if I give thee honour due,
Mirth, admit me of thy crew,
To live with her, and live with thee,
In unreprovèd pleasures free; 40
To hear the lark begin his flight,
And, singing, startle the dull night,
From his watch-tower in the skies,
Till the dappled dawn doth rise;
Then to come, in spite of sorrow, 45
And at my window bid good-morrow,
Through the sweet-briar or the vine,
Or the twisted eglantine;
While the cock, with lively din,
Scatters the rear of darkness thin; 50
And to the stack, or the barn-door,
Stoutly struts his dames before,

Oft listening how the hounds and horn
Cheerly rouse the slumbering morn,
From the side of some hoar hill,   55
Through the high wood echoing shrill.
Sometime walking, not unseen,
By hedgerow elms, on hillocks green,
Right against the eastern gate
Where the great sun begins his state,   60
Robed in flames and amber light,
The clouds in thousand liveries dight;
While the ploughman, near at hand,
Whistles o'er the furrowed land,
And the milkmaid singeth blithe,   65
And the mower whets his scythe,
And every shepherd tells his tale
Under the hawthorn in the dale.
Straight mine eye hath caught new pleasures,
Whilst the landscape round it measures: 70
Russet lawns, and fallows grey,
Where the nibbling flocks do stray;
Mountains on whose barren breast
The labouring clouds do often rest;
Meadows trim, with daisies pied,   75
Shallow brooks, and rivers wide.
Towers and battlements it sees
Bosomed high in tufted trees,
Where perhaps some beauty lies,
The cynosure of neighbouring eyes.   80
Hard by a cottage chimney smokes
From betwixt two aged oaks,
Where Corydon and Thyrsis met
Are at their savoury dinner set
Of herbs and other country messes,   85
Which the neat-handed Phyllis dresses;
And then in haste her bower she leaves,
With Thestylis to bind the sheaves;
Or, if the earlier season lead,
To the tanned haycock in the mead.   90
Sometimes, with secure delight,
The upland hamlets will invite,

When the merry bells ring round,
And the jocund rebecks sound
To many a youth and many a maid   95
Dancing in the chequered shade,
And young and old come forth to play
On a sunshine holiday,
Till the livelong daylight fail,
Then to a spicy nut-brown ale,   100
With stories told of many a feat,
How Fairy Mab the junkets eat;
She was pinched and pulled, she said,
And by the friar's lantern led,
Tells how the drudging goblin sweat   105
To earn his cream-bowl duly set,
When in one night, ere glimpse of morn,
His shadowy flail hath threshed the corn
That ten day-labourers could not end;
Then lies him down, the lubber fiend,   110
And, stretched out all the chimney's length
Basks at the fire his hairy strength,
And crop-full out of doors he flings,
Ere the first cock his matin rings.
Thus done the tales, to bed they creep,   115
By whispering winds soon lulled asleep.
Towered cities please us then,
And the busy hum of men,
Where throngs of knights and barons bold,
In weeds of peace, high triumphs hold,   120
With store of ladies, whose bright eyes
Rain influence, and judge the prize
Of wit or arms, while both contend
To win her grace whom all commend.
There let Hymen oft appear   125
In saffron robe, with taper clear,
And pomp, and feast, and revelry,
With mask and antique pageantry;
Such sights as youthful poets dream
On summer eves by haunted stream.   130
Then to the well-trod stage anon,
If Jonson's learned sock be on,

Or sweetest Shakespeare, Fancy's child,
Warble his native wood-notes wild.
And ever, against eating cares,   135
Lap me in soft Lydian airs,
Married to immortal verse,
Such as the meeting soul may pierce,
In notes with many a winding bout
Of linkèd sweetness long drawn out   140
With wanton heed and giddy cunning,
The melting voice through mazes running,
Untwisting all the chains that tie
The hidden soul of harmony.
That Orpheus' self may heave his head   145
From golden slumber on a bed
Of heaped Elysian flowers, and hear
Such strains as would have won the ear
Of Pluto to have quite set free
His half-regained Eurydice.   150
These delights if thou canst give,
Mirth, with thee I mean to live.

Il Penseroso

Hence, vain deluding Joys,
    The brood of Folly without father bred,
How little you bestead,
    Or fill the fixèd mind with all your toys;
Dwell in some idle brain,   5
    And fancies fond with gaudy shapes possess,
As thick and numberless
    As the gay motes that people the sunbeams,
Or likest hovering dreams,
    The fickle pensioners of Morpheus' train.   10
But, hail thou goddess, sage and holy,
Hail, divinest Melancholy,
Whose saintly visage is too bright

To hit the sense of human sight,
And therefore to our weaker view 15
O'erlaid with black, staid wisdom's hue.
Black, but such as in esteem
Prince Memnon's sister might beseem,
Or that starred Ethiop queen that strove
To set her beauty's praise above 20
The sea-nymphs, and their powers offended;
Yet thou art higher far descended,
Thee bright-haired Vesta long of yore
To solitary Saturn bore;
His daughter she (in Saturn's reign 25
Such mixture was not held a stain),
Oft in glimmering bowers and glades
He met her, and in secret shades
Of woody Ida's inmost grove,
Whilst yet there was no fear of Jove. 30
Come, pensive nun, devout and pure,
Sober, steadfast, and demure,
All in a robe of darkest grain,
Flowing with majestic train,
And sable stole of cypress lawn 35
Over thy decent shoulders drawn.
Come, but keep thy wonted state,
With even step, and musing gait,
And looks commercing with the skies,
Thy rapt soul sitting in thine eyes: 40
There, held in holy passion still,
Forget thyself to marble, till
With a sad leaden downward cast
Thou fix them on the earth as fast.
And join with thee calm Peace and Quiet, 45
Spare Fast, that oft with gods doth diet,
And hears the Muses in a ring
Aye round about Jove's altar sing.
And add to these retired Leisure,
That in trim gardens takes his pleasure; 50
But, first and chiefest, with thee bring
Him that yon soars on golden wing,

Guiding the fiery-wheelèd throne,
The cherub Contemplation;
And the mute Silence hist along,   55
'Less Philomel will deign a song,
In her sweetest saddest plight,
Smoothing the rugged brow of Night,
While Cynthia checks her dragon yoke
Gently o'er the accustomed oak.   60
Sweet bird, that shunn'st the noise of folly,
Most musical, most melancholy!
Thee, chauntress, oft the woods among
I woo, to hear thy even-song;
And, missing thee, I walk unseen   65
On the dry smooth-shaven green
To behold the wandering moon,
Riding near her highest noon,
Like one that had been led astray
Through the heaven's wide pathless way,   70
And oft, as if her head she bowed,
Stooping through a fleecy cloud.
Oft, on a plat of rising ground,
I hear the far-off curfew sound,
Over some wide-watered shore,   75
Swinging slow with sullen roar;
Or, if the air will not permit,
Some still removèd place will fit,
Where glowing embers through the room
Teach light to counterfeit a gloom,   80
Far from all resort of mirth,
Save the cricket on the hearth,
Or the bellman's drowsy charm
To bless the doors from nightly harm;
Or let my lamp, at midnight hour,   85
Be seen in some high lonely tower,
Where I may oft outwatch the Bear,
With thrice great Hermes, or unsphere
The spirit of Plato, to unfold
What worlds or what past regions hold   90
The immortal mind that hath forsook

Her mansion in this fleshly nook;
And of those demons that are found
In fire, air, flood, or underground,
Whose power hath a true consent   95
With planet or with element.
Sometimes let gorgeous Tragedy
In sceptered pall come sweeping by,
Presenting Thebes, or Pelops' line,
Or the tale of Troy divine,   100
Or what (though rare) of later age
Ennobled hath the buskined stage.
But, O sad Virgin, that thy power
Might raise Musaeus from his bower;
Or bid the soul of Orpheus sing   105
Such notes as, warbled to the string,
Drew iron tears down Pluto's cheek,
And made hell grant what love did seek;
Or call up him that left half-told
The story of Cambuscan bold,   110
Of Camball, and of Algarsife,
And who had Canace to wife,
That owned the virtuous ring and glass,
And of the wondrous horse of brass
On which the Tartar king did ride;   115
And if aught else great bards beside
In sage and solemn tunes have sung,
Of tourneys, and of trophies hung,
Of forests, and enchantments drear,
Where more is meant than meets the ear;   120
Thus, Night, oft see me in thy pale career,
Till civil-suited Morn appear,
Not tricked and frounced, as she was wont
With the Attic boy to hunt,
But kerchiefed in a comely cloud,   125
While rocking winds are piping loud,
Or ushered with a shower still,
When the gust hath blown his fill,
Ending on the rustling leaves,
With minute-drops from off the eaves.   130

And, when the sun begins to fling
His flaring beams, me, goddess, bring
To archèd walks of twilight groves,
And shadows brown, that Sylvan loves,
Of pine, or monumental oak,   135
Where the rude axe with heavèd stroke
Was never heard the nymphs to daunt,
Or fright them from their hallowed haunt.
There, in close covert, by some brook,
Where no profaner eye may look,   140
Hide me from day's garish eye,
While the bee with honeyed thigh,
That at her flowery work doth sing,
And the waters murmuring,
With such consort as they keep,   145
Entice the dewy-feathered Sleep;
And let some strange mysterious dream
Wave at his wings, in airy stream
Of lively portraiture displayed,
Softly on my eyelids laid;   150
And, as I wake, sweet music breathe
Above, about, or underneath,
Sent by some spirit to mortals good,
Or the unseen genius of the wood.
But let my due feet never fail   155
To walk the studious cloister's pale,
And love the high embowèd roof,
With antique pillars' massy-proof,
And storied windows richly dight,
Casting a dim religious light.   160
There let the pealing organ blow,
To the full-voiced choir below,
In service high and anthems clear,
As may with sweetness, through mine ear,
Dissolve me into ecstasies,   165
And bring all heaven before mine eyes.
And may at last my weary age
Find out the peaceful hermitage,
The hairy gown and mossy cell,

Where I may sit and rightly spell 170
Of every star that heaven doth show,
And every herb that sips the dew,
Till old experience do attain
To something like prophetic strain.
These pleasures, Melancholy, give; 175
And I with thee will choose to live.

Comus

The Persons

The ATTENDANT SPIRIT,	THE LADY.
afterwards in the habit	FIRST BROTHER.
of THYRSIS.	SECOND BROTHER.
COMUS, with his Crew.	SABRINA, the Nymph.

The Chief Persons which presented were:–

The Lord Brackley;
Mr Thomas Egerton, his Brother;
The Lady Alice Egerton.

The first Scene discovers a wild wood.
The ATTENDANT SPIRIT *descends or enters.*

Before the starry threshold of Jove's court
My mansion is, where those immortal shapes
Of bright aerial spirits live ensphered
In regions mild of calm and serene air,
Above the smoke and stir of this dim spot 5
Which men call earth, and, with low-thoughted care,
Confined and pestered in this pinfold here,
Strive to keep up a frail and feverish being
Unmindful of the crown that virtue gives,
After this mortal change, to her true servants 10
Amongst the enthronèd gods on sainted seats.

Yet some there be that by due steps aspire
To lay their just hands on that golden key
That opes the palace of eternity:
To such my errand is; and but for such,   15
I would not soil these pure ambrosial weeds
With the rank vapours of this sin-worn mould.
    But to my task. Neptune, besides the sway
Of every salt flood and each ebbing stream,
Took in by lot, 'twixt high and nether Jove,   20
Imperial rule of all the sea-girt isles
That, like to rich and various gems, inlay
The unadornèd bosom of the deep;
Which he, to grace his tributary gods,
By course commits to several government,   25
And gives them leave to wear their sapphire crowns
And wield their little tridents; but this isle,
The greatest and the best of all the main,
He quarters to his blue-haired deities;
And all this tract that fronts the falling sun   30
A noble peer of mickle trust and power
Has in his charge, with tempered awe to guide
An old and haughty nation, proud in arms:
Where his fair offspring, nursed in princely lore,
Are coming to attend their father's state,   35
And new-entrusted sceptre; but their way
Lies through the perplexed paths of this drear wood,
The nodding horror of whose shady brows
Threats the forlorn and wandering passenger;
And here their tender age might suffer peril,   40
But that, by quick command from sovereign Jove,
I was despatched for their defence and guard:
And listen why; for I will tell you now
What never yet was heard in tale or song,
From old or modern bard, in hall or bower.   45
    Bacchus, that first from out the purple grape
Crushed the sweet poison of misusèd wine,
After the Tuscan mariners transformed,
Coasting the Tyrrhene shore, as the winds listed,
On Circe's island fell. (Who knows not Circe,   50
The daughter of the Sun, whose charmèd cup

Whoever tasted lost his upright shape,
And downward fell into a grovelling swine?)
This Nymph, that gazed upon his clustering locks,
With ivy berries wreathed, and his blithe youth,   55
Had by him, ere he parted thence, a son
Much like his father, but his mother more,
Whom therefore she brought up, and Comus named:
Who, ripe and frolic of his full-grown age,
Roving the Celtic and Iberian fields,   60
At last betakes him to this ominous wood,
And, in thick shelter of black shades embowered,
Excels his mother at her mighty art,
Offering to every weary traveller
His orient liquor in a crystal glass,   65
To quench the drought of Phoebus; which as they taste
(For most do taste through fond intemperate thirst),
Soon as the potion works, their human countenance,
The express resemblance of the gods, is changed
Into some brutish form of wolf or bear,   70
Or ounce or tiger, hog, or bearded goat,
All other parts remaining as they were,
And they, so perfect in their misery,
Not once perceive their foul disfigurement,
But boast themselves more comely than before,   75
And all their friends and native home forget,
To roll with pleasure in a sensual sty.
Therefore, when any favoured of high Jove
Chances to pass through this adventurous glade,
Swift as the sparkle of a glancing star   80
I shoot from heaven, to give him safe convoy,
As now I do; but first I must put off
These my sky-robes, spun out of Iris' woof,
And take the weeds and likeness of a swain
That to the service of this house belongs,   85
Who, with his soft pipe and smooth-dittied song,
Well knows to still the wild winds when they roar,
And hush the waving woods; nor of less faith,
And in this office of his mountain watch
Likeliest, and nearest to the present aid   90
Of this occasion. But I hear the tread

Of hateful steps; I must be viewless now.

COMUS *enters, with a charming rod in one hand, his glass in the other;
with him a rout of monsters, headed like sundry sorts of wild beasts, but
otherwise like men and women, their apparel glistering; they come in,
making a riotous and unruly noise, with torches in their hands.*

COMUS. The star that bids the shepherd fold
Now the top of heaven doth hold;
And the gilded car of day   95
His glowing axle doth allay
In the steep Atlantic stream;
And the slope sun his upward beam
Shoots against the dusky pole,
Pacing toward the other goal   100
Of his chamber in the east.
Meanwhile, welcome joy and feast,
Midnight shout and revelry,
Tipsy dance and jollity.
Braid your locks with rosy twine,   105
Dropping odours, dropping wine.
Rigour now is gone to bed;
And Advice with scrupulous head,
Strict Age, and sour Severity,
With their grave saws, in slumber lie.   110
We, that are of purer fire,
Imitate the starry choir,
Who, in their nightly watchful spheres,
Lead in swift round the months and years.
The sounds and seas, with all their finny drove,   115
Now to the moon in wavering morris move;
And on the tawny sands and shelves
Trip the pert fairies and the dapper elves;
By dimpled brook and fountain-brim,
The wood-nymphs, decked with daisies trim,   120
Their merry wakes and pastimes keep:
What hath night to do with sleep?
Night hath better sweets to prove;
Venus now wakes, and wakens Love.
Come, let us our rites begin;   125
'Tis only daylight that makes sin,

Which these dun shades will ne'er report.
Hail, goddess of nocturnal sport,
Dark-veiled Cotytto, to whom the secret flame
Of midnight torches burns; mysterious dame,   130
That ne'er art called but when the dragon womb
Of Stygian darkness spits her thickest gloom,
And makes one blot of all the air;
Stay thy cloudy ebon chair,
Wherein thou ridest with Hecat', and befriend   135
Us thy vowed priests, till utmost end
Of all thy dues be done, and none left out;
Ere the blabbing eastern scout,
The nice Morn on the Indian steep,
From her cabined loop-hole peep,   140
And to the tell-tale Sun descry
Our concealed solemnity.
Come, knit hands, and beat the ground
In a light fantastic round.

The Measure.

Break off, break off! I feel the different pace   145
Of some chaste footing near about this ground.
Run to your shrouds within these brakes and trees;
Our number may affright: some virgin sure
(For so I can distinguish by mine art)
Benighted in these woods! Now to my charms,   150
And to my wily trains; I shall ere long
Be well stocked with as fair a herd as grazed
About my mother Circe. Thus I hurl
My dazzling spells into the spongy air,
Of power to cheat the eye with blear illusion,   155
And give it false presentments, lest the place
And my quaint habits breed astonishment,
And put the damsel to suspicious flight:
Which must not be, for that's against my course.
I, under fair pretence of friendly ends,   160
And well-placed words of glozing courtesy,
Baited with reasons not unplausible,
Wind me into the easy-hearted man,
And hug him into snares. When once her eye
Hath met the virtue of this magic dust,   165

I shall appear some harmless villager
Whom thrift keeps up about his country gear.
But here she comes; I fairly step aside,
And hearken, if I may her business hear.

THE LADY *enters.*

LADY. This way the noise was, if mine ear be true,   170
My best guide now; methought it was the sound
Of riot and ill-managed merriment,
Such as the jocund flute or gamesome pipe
Stirs up among the loose unlettered hinds,
When, for their teeming flocks and granges full,   175
In wanton dance they praise the bounteous Pan,
And thank the gods amiss. I should be loath
To meet the rudeness and swilled insolence
Of such late wassailers; yet O where else
Shall I inform my unacquainted feet   180
In the blind mazes of this tangled wood?
My brothers, when they saw me wearied out
With this long way, resolving here to lodge
Under the spreading favour of these pines,
Stepped, as they said, to the next thicket-side   185
To bring me berries, or such cooling fruit
As the kind hospitable woods provide.
They left me then when the grey-hooded Even,
Like a sad votarist in palmer's weed,
Rose from the hindmost wheels of Phoebus' wain.   190
But where they are, and why they came not back,
Is now the labour of my thoughts; 'tis likeliest
They had engaged their wandering steps too far;
And envious darkness, ere they could return,
Had stole them from me: else, O thievish Night,   195
Why shouldst thou, but for some felonious end,
In thy dark lantern thus close up the stars
That Nature hung in heaven, and filled their lamps
With everlasting oil to give due light
To the misled and lonely traveller?   200
This is the place, as well as I may guess,
Whence even now the tumult of loud mirth
Was rife, and perfect in my listening ear;

Yet nought but single darkness do I find.
What might this be? A thousand fantasies   205
Begin to throng into my memory,
Of calling shapes, and beckoning shadows dire,
And airy tongues that syllable men's names
On sands and shores and desert wildernesses.
These thoughts may startle well, but not astound 210
The virtuous mind, that ever walks attended
By a strong siding champion, Conscience. . . .
O welcome pure-eyed Faith, white-handed Hope,
Thou hovering angel girt with golden wings,
And thou unblemished form of Chastity!   215
I see ye visibly, and now believe
That he, the Supreme Good, to whom all things ill
Are but as slavish officers of vengeance,
Would send a glistering guardian, if need were,
To keep my life and honour unassailed.   220
Was I deceived, or did a sable cloud
Turn forth her silver lining on the night?
I did not err: there does a sable cloud
Turn forth her silver lining on the night,
And casts a gleam over this tufted grove.   225
I cannot hallo to my brothers, but
Such noise as I can make to be heard farthest
I'll venture, for my new-enlivened spirits
Prompt me; and they perhaps are not far off.

SONG

Sweet Echo, sweetest nymph, that liv'st unseen   230
        Within thy airy shell
    By slow Meander's margent green,
And in the violet-embroidered vale
        Where the love-lorn nightingale
Nightly to thee her sad song mourneth well: 235
Canst thou not tell me of a gentle pair
        That likest thy Narcissus are?
        O, if thou have
    Hid them in some flowery cave,
        Tell me but where,   240
    Sweet queen of parley, daughter of the sphere!

So may'st thou be translated to the skies,
And give resounding grace to all heaven's harmonies.

COMUS. Can any mortal mixture of earth's mould
Breathe such divine enchanting ravishment?   245
Sure something holy lodges in that breast,
And with these raptures moves the vocal air
To testify his hidden residence;
How sweetly did they float upon the wings
Of silence, through the empty-vaulted night,   250
At every fall smoothing the raven down
Of darkness till it smiled; I have oft heard
My mother Circe with the Sirens three,
Amidst the flowery-kirtled Naiades,
Culling their potent herbs and baleful drugs,   255
Who, as they sung, would take the prisoned soul,
And lap it in Elysium; Scylla wept,
And chid her barking waves into attention,
And fell Charybdis murmured soft applause;
Yet they in pleasing slumber lulled the sense,   260
And in sweet madness robbed it of itself;
But such a sacred and home-felt delight,
Such sober certainty of waking bliss,
I never heard till now. I'll speak to her,
And she shall be my queen. – Hail, foreign wonder!   265
Whom certain these rough shades did never breed,
Unless the goddess that in rural shrine
Dwell'st here with Pan or Sylvan, by blest song,
Forbidding every bleak unkindly fog
To touch the prosperous growth of this tall wood.   270
LADY. Nay, gentle shepherd, ill is lost that praise
That is addressed to unattending ears;
Not any boast of skill, but extreme shift
How to regain my severed company,
Compelled me to awake the courteous Echo   275
To give me answer from her mossy couch.
COMUS. What chance, good Lady, hath bereft you thus?
LADY. Dim darkness and this leafy labyrinth.
COMUS. Could that divide you from near-ushering guides?
LADY. They left me weary on a grassy turf.   280

COMUS. By falsehood, or discourtesy, or why?
LADY. To seek i' the valley some cool friendly spring.
COMUS. And left your fair side all unguarded, Lady?
LADY. They were but twain, and purposed quick return.
COMUS. Perhaps forestalling night prevented them. 285
LADY. How easy my misfortune is to hit!
COMUS. Imports their loss, beside the present need?
LADY. No less than if I should my brothers lose.
COMUS. Were they of manly prime, or youthful bloom?
LADY. As smooth as Hebe's their unrazored lips. 290
COMUS. Two such I saw, what time the laboured ox
In his loose traces from the furrow came,
And the swinked hedger at his supper sat.
I saw them under a green mantling vine,
That crawls along the side of yon small hill, 295
Plucking ripe clusters from the tender shoots;
Their port was more than human, as they stood.
I took it for a fairy vision
Of some gay creatures of the element,
That in the colours of the rainbow live, 300
And play i' the plighted clouds. I was awe-struck,
And, as I passed, I worshipped; if those you seek,
It were a journey like the path to heaven
To help you find them.
LADY.   Gentle villager, 305
What readiest way would bring me to that place?
COMUS. Due west it rises from this shrubby point.
LADY. To find out that, good shepherd, I suppose,
In such a scant allowance of star-light,
Would overtask the best land-pilot's art,
Without the sure guess of well-practised feet. 310
COMUS. I know each lane, and every alley green,
Dingle, or bushy dell, of this wild wood,
And every bosky bourn from side to side,
My daily walks and ancient neighbourhood;
And, if your stray attendance be yet lodged, 315
Or shroud within these limits, I shall know
Ere morrow wake, or the low-roosted lark
From her thatched pallet rouse. If otherwise,
I can conduct you, Lady, to a low

But loyal cottage, where you may be safe   320
Till further quest.
    LADY.   Shepherd, I take thy word,
And trust thy honest-offered courtesy,
Which oft is sooner found in lowly sheds,
With smoky rafters, than in tapestry halls   325
And courts of princes, where it first was named,
And yet is most pretended: in a place
Less warranted than this, or less secure,
I cannot be, that I should fear to change it.
Eye me, blest Providence, and square my trial
To my proportioned strength! Shepherd, lead on. . . .   330

The TWO BROTHERS.

    ELD. BRO. Unmuffle, ye faint stars; and thou, fair moon,
That wont'st to love the traveller's benison,
Stoop thy pale visage through an amber cloud,
And disinherit Chaos, that reigns here
In double night of darkness and of shades;   335
Or, if your influence be quite dammed up
With black usurping mists, some gentle taper,
Though a rush-candle from the wicker hole
Or some clay habitation, visit us
With thy long levelled rule of streaming light,   340
And thou shalt be our Star of Arcady,
Or Tyrian Cynosure.
    SEC. BRO.   Or, if our eyes
Be barred that happiness, might we but hear
The folded flocks, penned in their wattled cotes,   345
Or sound of pastoral reed with oaten stops,
Or whistle from the lodge, or village cock
Count the night-watches to his feathery dames,
'Twould be some solace yet, some little cheering,
In this close dungeon of innumerous boughs.
But, O, that hapless virgin, our lost sister!   350
Where may she wander now, whither betake her
From the chill dew, amongst rude burs and thistles?
Perhaps some cold bank is her bolster now,
Or 'gainst the rugged bark of some broad elm
Leans her unpillowed head, fraught with sad fears.   355

What if in wild amazement and affright,
Or, while we speak, within the direful grasp
Of savage hunger, or of savage heat!
   ELD. BRO. Peace, brother: be not over-exquisite
To cast the fashion of uncertain evils;   360
For, grant they be so, while they rest unknown,
What need a man forestall his date of grief,
And run to meet what he would most avoid?
Or, if they be but false alarms of fear,
How bitter is such self-delusion!   365
I do not think my sister so to seek,
Or so unprincipled in virtue's book,
And the sweet peace that goodness bosoms ever,
As that the single want of light and noise
(Not being in danger, as I trust she is not)   370
Could stir the constant mood of her calm thoughts,
And put them into misbecoming plight.
Virtue could see to do what Virtue would
By her own radiant light, though sun and moon
Were in the flat sea sunk. And Wisdom's self   375
Oft seeks to sweet retired solitude,
Where, with her best nurse, Contemplation,
She plumes her feathers, and lets grow her wings,
That, in the various bustle of resort,
Were all to-ruffled, and sometimes impaired.   380
He that has light within his own clear breast
May sit i' the centre, and enjoy bright day;
But he that hides a dark soul and foul thoughts
Benighted walks under the mid-day sun;
Himself is his own dungeon.
   SEC. BRO.   'Tis most true   385
That musing Meditation most affects
The pensive secrecy of desert cell,
Far from the cheerful haunt of men and herds,
And sits as safe as in a senate-house;
For who would rob a hermit of his weeds,   390
His few books, or his beads, or maple dish,
Or do his grey hairs any violence?
But Beauty, like the fair Hesperian tree
Laden with blooming gold, had need the guard

Of dragon-watch with unenchanted eye   395
To save her blossoms, and defend her fruit,
From the rash hand of bold Incontinence.
You may as well spread out the unsunned heaps
Of miser's treasure by an outlaw's den,
And tell me it is safe, as bid me hope   400
Danger will wink on Opportunity,
And let a single helpless maiden pass
Uninjured in this wild surrounding waste.
Of night or loneliness it recks me not;
I fear the dread events that dog them both,   405
Lest some ill-greeting touch attempt the person
Of our unownèd sister.
    ELD. BRO.   I do not, brother,
Infer as if I thought my sister's state
Secure without all doubt or controversy;
Yet, where an equal poise of hope and fear   410
Does arbitrate the event, my nature is
That I incline to hope rather than fear,
And gladly banish squint suspicion.
My sister is not so defenceless left
As you imagine; she has a hidden strength,   415
Which you remember not.
    SEC. BRO.   What hidden strength,
Unless the strength of heaven, if you mean that?
    ELD. BRO. I mean that too, but yet a hidden strength,
Which, if heaven gave it, may be termed her own.
'Tis chastity, my brother, chastity: 420
She that has that is clad in complete steel,
And, like a quivered nymph with arrows keen,
May trace huge forests, and unharboured heaths,
Infamous hills, and sandy perilous wilds;
Where, through the sacred rays of chastity,   425
No savage fierce, bandit, or mountaineer,
Will dare to soil her virgin purity.
Yea, there where very desolation dwells,
By grots and caverns shagged with horrid shades,
She may pass on with unblenched majesty,   430
Be it not done in pride, or in presumption.
Some say no evil thing that walks by night,

In fog or fire, by lake or moorish fen,
Blue meagre hag, or stubborn unlaid ghost,
That breaks his magic chains at curfew time,   435
No goblin or swart fairy of the mine,
Hath hurtful power o'er true virginity.
Do ye believe me yet, or shall I call
Antiquity from the old schools of Greece
To testify the arms of chastity?   440
Hence had the huntress Dian her dread bow,
Fair silver-shafted queen for ever chaste,
Wherewith she tamed the brinded lioness
And spotted mountain-pard, but set at nought
The frivolous bow of Cupid; gods and men   445
Feared her stern frown, and she was queen o' the woods.
What was the snaky-headed Gorgon shield
That wise Minerva wore, unconquered virgin,
Wherewith she freezed her foes to congealed stone,
But rigid looks of chaste austerity,   450
And noble grace that dashed brute violence
With sudden adoration and blank awe?
So dear to heaven is saintly chastity
That, when a soul is found sincerely so,
A thousand liveried angels lackey her,   455
Driving far off each thing of sin and guilt,
And in clear dream and solemn vision
Tell her of things that no gross ear can hear;
Till oft converse with heavenly habitants
Begin to cast a beam on the outward shape,   460
The unpolluted temple of the mind,
And turns it by degrees to the soul's essence,
Till all be made immortal. But when lust,
By unchaste looks, loose gestures, and foul talk,
But most by lewd and lavish act of sin,   465
Lets in defilement to the inward parts,
The soul grows clotted by contagion,
Embodies, and imbrutes, till she quite lose
The divine property of her first being.
Such are those thick and gloomy shadows damp   470
Oft seen in charnel-vaults and sepulchres,
Lingering and sitting by a new-made grave,

As loath to leave the body that it loved,
And linked itself by carnal sensualty
To a degenerate and degraded state.   475
    SEC. BRO. How charming is divine philosophy!
Not harsh and crabbed, as dull fools suppose,
But musical as is Apollo's lute,
And a perpetual feast of nectared sweets,
Where no crude surfeit reigns.
    ELD. BRO.   List! list! I hear   480
Some far-off hallo break the silent air.
    SEC. BRO. Methought so too; what should it be?
    ELD. BRO.   For certain,
Either some one, like us, night-foundered here,
Or else some neighbour woodman, or, at worst,
Some roving robber calling to his fellows.   485
    SEC. BRO. Heaven keep my sister! Again, again, and near!
Best draw, and stand upon our guard.
ELD. BRO.   I'll hallo.
If he be friendly, he comes well; if not,
Defence is a good cause, and heaven be for us!

> *The* ATTENDANT SPIRIT, *habited like a shepherd.*

That hallo I should know. What are you? Speak.   490
Come not too near; you fall on iron stakes else.
    SPIR. What voice is that? My young Lord? Speak again.
    SEC. BRO. O brother, 'tis my father's shepherd, sure.
    ELD. BRO. Thyrsis? Whose artful strains have oft delayed
The huddling brook to hear his madrigal,   495
And sweetened every musk-rose of the dale,
How camest thou here, good swain? Hath any ram
Slipped from the fold, or young kid lost his dam,
Or straggling wether the pent flock forsook?
How couldst thou find this dark sequestered nook?   500
    SPIR. O my loved master's heir, and his next joy,
I came not here on such a trivial toy
As a strayed ewe, or to pursue the stealth
Of pilfering wolf; not all the fleecy wealth
That doth enrich these downs is worth a thought   505
To this my errand, and the care it brought.
But O my virgin Lady, where is she?

How chance she is not in your company?

ELD. BRO. To tell thee sadly, shepherd, without blame
Or our neglect, we lost her as we came.   510

SPIR. Ay me unhappy! Then my fears are true.

ELD. BRO. What fears, good Thyrsis? Prithee briefly show,

SPIR. I'll tell ye; 'tis not vain or fabulous
(Though so esteemed by shallow ignorance)
What the sage poets, taught by the heavenly Muse,   515
Storied of old in high immortal verse
Of dire chimeras and enchanted isles,
And rifted rocks whose entrance leads to hell;
For such there be, but unbelief is blind.

Within the navel of this hideous wood,   520
Immured in cypress shades, a sorcerer dwells,
Of Bacchus and of Circe born, great Comus,
Deep skilled in all his mother's witcheries,
And here to every thirsty wanderer
By sly enticement gives his baneful cup,   525
With many murmurs mixed, whose pleasing poison
The visage quite transforms of him that drinks,
And the inglorious likeness of a beast
Fixes instead, unmoulding reason's mintage
Charactered in the face; this have I learnt   530
Tending my flocks hard by i' the hilly crofts
That brow this bottom glade, whence night by night
He and his monstrous rout are heard to howl
Like stabled wolves, or tigers at their prey,
Doing abhorred rites to Hecate   535
In their obscurèd haunts of inmost bowers;
Yet have they many baits and guileful spells
To inveigle and invite the unwary sense
Of them that pass unweeting by the way.
This evening late, by then the chewing flocks   540
Had ta'en their supper on the savoury herb
Of knot-grass dew-besprent, and were in fold,
I sat me down to watch upon a bank
With ivy canopied, and interwove
With flaunting honeysuckle, and began,   545
Wrapped in a pleasing fit of melancholy,
To meditate my rural minstrelsy,

Till fancy had her fill; but ere a close
The wonted roar was up amidst the woods,
And filled the air with barbarous dissonance   550
At which I ceased, and listened them a while,
Till an unusual stop of sudden silence
Gave respite to the drowsy-flighted steeds
That draw the litter of close-curtained sleep.
At last a soft and solemn-breathing sound   555
Rose like a steam of rich distilled perfumes,
And stole upon the air, that even Silence
Was took ere she was ware, and wished she might
Deny her nature, and be never more,
Still to be so displaced. I was all ear,   560
And took in strains that might create a soul
Under the ribs of Death. But O ere long
Too well I did perceive it was the voice
Of my most honoured Lady, your dear sister.
Amazed I stood, harrowed with grief and fear;   565
And 'O poor hapless nightingale,' thought I,
'How sweet thou sing'st, how near the deadly snare!'
Then down the lawns I ran with headlong haste,
Through paths and turnings often trod by day,
Till, guided by mine ear, I found the place   570
Where that damned wizard, hid in sly disguise
(For so by certain signs I knew), had met
Already, ere my best speed could prevent,
The aidless innocent Lady, his wished prey,
Who gently asked if he had seen such two,   575
Supposing him some neighbour villager;
Longer I durst not stay, but soon I guessed
Ye were the two she meant; with that I sprung
Into swift flight, till I had found you here;
But further know I not.
    SEC. BRO.   O night and shades,   580
How are ye joined with hell in triple knot
Against the unarmed weakness of one virgin,
Alone and helpless! Is this the confidence
You gave me, brother?
    ELD. BRO.   Yes, and keep it still:
Lean on it safely: not a period   585

Shall be unsaid for me. Against the threats
Of malice or of sorcery, or that power
Which erring men call chance, this I hold firm:
Virtue may be assailed, but never hurt,
Surprised by unjust force, but not enthralled;   590
Yea, even that which mischief meant most harm
Shall in the happy trial prove most glory.
But evil on itself shall back recoil,
And mix no more with goodness, when at last,
Gathered like scum, and settled to itself,   595
It shall be in eternal restless change
Self-fed and self-consumed. If this fail,
The pillared firmament is rottenness,
And earth's base built on stubble. But come, let's on!
Against the opposing will and arm of heaven   600
May never this just sword be lifted up;
But, for that damned magician, let him be girt
With all the grisly legions that troop
Under the sooty flag of Acheron,
Harpies and Hydras, or all the monstrous forms   605
'Twixt Africa and Ind, I'll find him out,
And force him to return his purchase back,
Or drag him by the curls to a foul death,
Cursed as his life.
   SPIR.   Alas, good venturous youth,   610
I love thy courage yet, and bold emprise;
But here thy sword can do thee little stead;
Far other arms and other weapons must
Be those that quell the might of hellish charms;
He with his bare wand can unthread thy joints,
And crumble all thy sinews.   615
   ELD. BRO.   Why, prithee, shepherd,
How durst thou then thyself approach so near
As to make this relation?
   SPIR.   Care and utmost shifts
How to secure the lady from surprisal
Brought to my mind a certain shepherd lad
Of small regard to see to, yet well skilled   620
In every virtuous plant and healing herb
That spreads her verdant leaf to the morning ray;

He loved me well, and oft would beg me sing,
Which when I did, he on the tender grass
Would sit, and hearken even to ecstasy,   625
And in requital ope his leathern scrip,
And show me simples of a thousand names,
Telling their strange and vigorous faculties;
Amongst the rest a small unsightly root,
But of divine effect, he culled me out;   630
The leaf was darkish, and had prickles on it,
But in another country, as he said,
Bore a bright golden flower, but not in this soil:
Unknown, and like esteemed, and the dull swain
Treads on it daily with his clouted shoon;   635
And yet more med'cinal is it than that moly
That Hermes once to wise Ulysses gave.
He called it haemony, and gave it me,
And bade me keep it as of sovereign use
'Gainst all enchantments, mildew blast, or damp,   640
Or ghastly Furies' apparition;
I pursed it up, but little reckoning made,
Till now that this extremity compelled,
But now I find it true; for by this means
I knew the foul enchanter, though disguised,   645
Entered the very lime-twigs of his spells,
And yet came off. If you have this about you
(As I will give you when we go) you may
Boldly assault the necromancer's hall;
Where if he be, with dauntless hardihood   650
And brandished blade rush on him, break his glass,
And shed the luscious liquid on the ground,
But seize his wand; though he and his cursed crew
Fierce sign of battle make, and menace high,
Or like the sons of Vulcan, vomit smoke,   655
Yet will they soon retire, if he but shrink.
   ELD. BRO. Thyrsis, lead on apace; I'll follow thee,
And some good angel bear a shield before us!

*The scene changes to a stately palace, set out with all manner of
deliciousness: soft music, tables spread with all dainties.* COMUS *appears
with his rabble, and* THE LADY *set in an enchanted chair: to whom he
offers his glass, which she puts by, and goes about to rise.*

COMUS. Nay, Lady, sit. If I but wave this wand,
Your nerves are all chained up in alabaster, 660
And you a statue, or as Daphne was,
Root-bound, that fled Apollo.
LADY.   Fool, do not boast;
Thou canst not touch the freedom of my mind
With all thy charms, although this corporal rind
Thou hast immanacled while heaven sees good. 665
COMUS. Why are you vexed, Lady? Why do you frown?
Here dwell no frowns, nor anger; from these gates
Sorrow flies far. See, here be all the pleasures
That fancy can beget on youthful thoughts,
When the fresh blood grows lively, and returns 670
Brisk as the April buds in primrose season.
And first behold this cordial julep here,
That flames and dances in his crystal bounds,
With spirits of balm and fragrant syrups mixed.
Not that Nepenthes which the wife of Thone 675
In Egypt gave to Jove-born Helena
Is of such power to stir up joy as this,
To life so friendly, or so cool to thirst.
Why should you be so cruel to yourself,
And to those dainty limbs, which Nature lent 680
For gentle usage and soft delicacy?
But you invert the covenants of her trust,
And harshly deal, like an ill borrower,
With that which you received on other terms,
Scorning the unexempt condition 685
By which all mortal frailty must subsist,
Refreshment after toil, ease after pain,
That have been tired all day without repast,
And timely rest have wanted. But, fair virgin,
This will restore all soon.
LADY.   'Twill not, false traitor! 690
'Twill not restore the truth and honesty
That thou hast banished from thy tongue with lies;
Was this the cottage and the safe abode
Thou told'st me of? What grim aspects are these,
These ugly-headed monsters? Mercy guard me! 695
Hence with thy brewed enchantments, foul deceiver!

Hast thou betrayed my credulous innocence
With vizored falsehood and base forgery?
And would'st thou seek again to trap me here
With liquorish baits, fit to ensnare a brute?   700
Were it a draught for Juno when she banquets,
I would not taste thy treasonous offer; none
But such as are good men can give good things,
And that which is not good is not delicious
To a well-governed and wise appetite.   705
   COMUS. O foolishness of men! That lend their ears
To those budge doctors of the Stoic fur,
And fetch their precepts from the Cynic tub,
Praising the lean and sallow Abstinence!
Wherefore did Nature pour her bounties forth   710
With such a full and unwithdrawing hand,
Covering the earth with odours, fruits, and flocks,
Thronging the seas with spawn innumerable,
But all to please and sate the curious taste?
And set to work millions of spinning worms,   715
That in their green shops weave the smooth-haired silk,
To deck her sons; and, that no corner might
Be vacant of her plenty, in her own loins
She hutched the all-worshipped ore and precious gems,
To store her children with; if all the world   720
Should, in a pet of temperance, feed on pulse,
Drink the clear stream, and nothing wear but frieze,
The all-giver would be unthanked, would be unpraised,
Not half his riches known, and yet despised;
And we should serve him as a grudging master,   725
As a penurious niggard of his wealth,
And live like Nature's bastards, not her sons,
Who would be quite surcharged with her own weight,
And strangled with her waste fertility:
The earth cumbered, and the winged air darked with plumes,   730
The herds would over-multitude their lords,
The sea o'erfraught would swell, and the unsought diamonds
Would so emblaze the forehead of the deep,
And so bestud with stars, that they below
Would grow inured to light, and come at last   735
To gaze upon the sun with shameless brows.

List, Lady; be not coy, and be not cozened
With that same vaunted name, Virginity.
Beauty is Nature's coin; must not be hoarded,
But must be current; and the good thereof   740
Consists in mutual and partaken bliss,
Unsavoury in the enjoyment of itself.
If you let slip time, like a neglected rose
It withers on the stalk with languished head.
Beauty is Nature's brag, and must be shown   745
In courts, at feasts, and high solemnities,
Where most may wonder at the workmanship.
It is for homely features to keep home;
They had their name thence: coarse complexions
And cheeks of sorry grain will serve to ply   750
The sampler, and to tease the housewife's wool.
What need a vermeil-tinctured lip for that,
Love-darting eyes, or tresses like the morn?
There was another meaning in these gifts;
Think what, and be advised; you are but young yet.   755
    LADY. I had not thought to have unlocked my lips
In this unhallowed air, but that this juggler
Would think to charm my judgement, as mine eyes,
Obtruding false rules pranked in reason's garb.
I hate when vice can bolt her arguments   760
And virtue has no tongue to check her pride.
Impostor! Do not charge most innocent Nature,
As if she would her children should be riotous
With her abundance. She, good cateress,
Means her provision only to the good,   765
That live according to her sober laws,
And holy dictate of spare Temperance.
If every just man that now pines with want
Had but a moderate and beseeming share
Of that which lewdly-pampered Luxury   770
Now heaps upon some few with vast excess,
Nature's full blessings would be well-dispensed
In unsuperfluous even proportion,
And she no whit encumbered with her store;
And then the giver would be better thanked   775
His praise due paid: for swinish gluttony

Ne'er looks to heaven amidst his gorgeous feast,
But with besotted base ingratitude
Crams, and blasphemes his feeder. Shall I go on?
Or have I said enough? To him that dares   780
Arm his profane tongue with contemptuous words
Against the sun-clad power of chastity
Fain would I something say – yet to what end?
Thou hast nor ear, nor soul, to apprehend
The sublime notion and high mystery   785
That must be uttered to unfold the sage
And serious doctrine of Virginity;
And thou art worthy that thou shouldst not know
More happiness than this thy present lot.
Enjoy your dear wit, and gay rhetoric,   790
That hath so well been taught her dazzling fence;
Thou art not fit to hear thyself convinced.
Yet, should I try, the uncontrollèd worth
Of this pure cause would kindle my rapt spirits
To such a flame of sacred vehemence   795
That dumb things would be moved to sympathise,
And the brute Earth would lend her nerves, and shake,
Till all thy magic structures, reared so high,
Were shattered into heaps o'er thy false head.
   COMUS. She fables not. I feel that I do fear   800
Her words set off by some superior power;
And, though not mortal, yet a cold shuddering dew
Dips me all o'er, as when the wrath of Jove
Speaks thunder and the chains of Erebus
To some of Saturn's crew. I must dissemble,   805
And try her yet more strongly. Come, no more!
This is mere moral babble, and direct
Against the canon laws of our foundation.
I must not suffer this; yet 'tis but the lees
And settlings of a melancholy blood.   810
But this will cure all straight; one sip of this
Will bathe the drooping spirits in delight
Beyond the bliss of dreams. Be wise, and taste. . . .

The BROTHERS *rush in with swords drawn, wrest his glass out of his
hand, and break it against the ground; his rout make sign of resistance,
but are all driven in. The* ATTENDANT SPIRIT *comes in.*

SPIR. What! Have you let the false enchanter scape?
O ye mistook; ye should have snatched his wand,   815
And bound him fast. Without his rod reversed,
And backward mutters of dissevering power,
We cannot free the Lady that sits here
In stony fetters fixed and motionless.
Yet stay: be not disturbed; now I bethink me,   820
Some other means I have which may be used,
Which once of Meliboeus old I learnt,
The soothest shepherd that e'er piped on plains.
    There is a gentle Nymph not far from hence,
That with moist curb sways the smooth Severn stream: 825
Sabrina is her name, a virgin pure;
Whilom she was the daughter of Locrine,
That had the sceptre from his father Brute.
She, guileless damsel, flying the mad pursuit
Of her enragèd stepdame, Guendolen,   830
Commended her fair innocence to the flood
That stayed her flight with his cross-flowing course;
The water-nymphs, that in the bottom played,
Held up their pearled wrists, and took her in,
Bearing her straight to aged Nereus' hall,   835
Who, piteous of her woes, reared her lank head,
And gave her to his daughters to imbathe
In nectared lavers strewed with asphodel,
And through the porch and inlet of each sense
Dropped in ambrosial oils, till she revived,   840
And underwent a quick immortal change,
Made goddess of the river; still she retains
Her maiden gentleness, and oft at eve
Visits the herds along the twilight meadows,
Helping all urchin blasts, and ill-luck signs   845
That the shrewd meddling of elf delights to make,
Which she with precious vialed liquors heals.
For which the shepherds at their festivals
Carol her goodness loud in rustic lays,
And throw sweet garland wreaths into her stream   850
Of pansies, pinks, and gaudy daffodils.
And, as the old swain said, she can unlock
The clasping charm, and thaw the numbing spell,

If she be right invoked in warbled song;
For maidenhood she loves, and will be swift   855
To aid a virgin, such as was herself,
In hard-besetting need; this will I try,
And add the power of some adjuring verse.

                              SONG
Sabrina fair,
    Listen where thou art sitting   860
Under the glassy, cool, translucent wave,
    In twisted braids of lilies knitting
The loose train of thy amber-dropping hair;
    Listen for dear honour's sake,   865
    Goddess of the silver lake,
        Listen and save.

Listen, and appear to us,
In name of great Oceanus.
By the earth-shaking Neptune's mace,
And Tethys' grave majestic pace;   870
By hoary Nereus' wrinkled look,
And the Carpathian wizard's hook;
By scaly Triton's winding shell,
And old soothsaying Glaucus' spell;
By Leucothea's lovely hands,   875
And her son that rules the strands;
By Thetis' tinsel-slippered feet,
And the songs of Sirens sweet;
By dead Parthenope's dear tomb,
And fair Ligea's golden comb,   880
Wherewith she sits on diamond rocks
Sleeking her soft alluring locks;
By all the Nymphs that nightly dance
Upon thy streams with wily glance;
Rise, rise, and heave thy rosy head   885
From thy coral-paven bed,
And bridle in thy headlong wave,
Till thou our summons answered have.
                        Listen and save.

SABRINA *rises, attended by water-nymphs, and sings.*

By the rushy-fringèd bank,   890
Where grows the willow and the osier dank,
  My sliding chariot stays,
Thick set with agate, and the azurn sheen
Of turkis blue, and emerald green,
  That in the channel strays: 890
Whilst from off the waters fleet
Thus I set my printless feet
O'er the cowslip's velvet head,
  That bends not as I tread.
Gentle swain, at thy request
  I am here.   900
  SPIR. Goddess dear,
We implore thy powerful hand
To undo the charmèd band
Of true virgin here distressed   905
Through the force and through the wile
Of unblessed enchanter vile.
  SABR. Shepherd, 'tis my office best
To help ensnarèd chastity.
Brightest Lady, look on me.   910
Thus I sprinkle on thy breast
Drops that from my fountain pure
I have kept of precious cure;
Thrice upon thy finger's tip,
Thrice upon thy rubied lip: 915
Next this marble venomed seat,
Smeared with gums of glutinous heat,
I touch with chaste palms moist and cold.
Now the spell hath lost his hold;
And I must haste ere morning hour   920
To wait in Amphitrite's bower.

SABRINA *descends, and* THE LADY *rises out of her seat.*

  SPIR. Virgin, daughter of Locrine,
Sprung of old Anchises' line,
May thy brimmèd waves for this
Their full tribute never miss   925
From a thousand petty rills,
That tumble down the snowy hills;

Summer drought or singèd air
Never scorch thy tresses fair,
Nor wet October's torrent flood   930
Thy molten crystal fill with mud;
May thy billows roll ashore
The beryl and the golden ore;
May thy lofty head be crowned
With many a tower and terrace round,   930
And here and there thy banks upon
With groves of myrrh and cinnamon.
Come, Lady; while heaven lends us grace,
Let us fly this cursed place,
Lest the sorcerer us entice   940
With some other new device.
Not a waste or needless sound
Till we come to holier ground.
I shall be your faithful guide
Through this gloomy covert wide;   945
And not many furlongs thence
Is your father's residence,
Where this night are met in state
Many a friend to gratulate
His wished presence, and beside   950
All the swains that there abide
With jigs and rural dance resort;
We shall catch them at their sport,
And our sudden coming there
Will double all their mirth and cheer.   955
Come, let us haste; the stars grow high,
But Night sits monarch yet in the mid sky.

*The Scene changes, presenting Ludlow Town, and the President's Castle:
then come in country dancers; after them the* ATTENDANT SPIRIT, *with
the two* BROTHERS *and* THE LADY.

SONG
   SPIR. Back, shepherds, back! Enough your play
Till next sun-shine holiday.
Here be, without duck or nod,   960
Other trippings to be trod
Of lighter toes, and such court guise

As Mercury did first devise
With the mincing Dryades
On the lawns and on the leas.   965

This second Song presents them to their Father and Mother.

  Noble Lord and Lady bright,
I have brought ye new delight.
Here behold so goodly grown
Three fair branches of your own;
Heaven hath timely tried their youth,   970
Their faith, their patience, and their truth,
And sent them here through hard assays
With a crown of deathless praise,
To triumph in victorious dance
O'er sensual folly and intemperance.   975

The dances ended, the SPIRIT *epiloguizes.*

  SPIR. To the ocean now I fly,
And those happy climes that lie
Where day never shuts his eye,
Up in the broad fields of the sky;
There I suck the liquid air,   980
All amidst the gardens fair
Of Hesperus, and his daughters three
That sing about the golden tree.
Along the crispèd shades and bowers
Revels the spruce and jocund Spring;   985
The Graces and the rosy-bosomed Hours
Thither all their bounties bring.
There eternal summer dwells,
And west winds with musky wing
About the cedarn alleys fling   990
Nard and cassia's balmy smells.
Iris there with humid bow
Waters the odorous banks, that blow
Flowers of more mingled hue
Than her purfled scarf can show,   995
And drenches with Elysian dew
(List, mortals, if your ears be true)
Beds of hyacinth and roses,

Where young Adonis oft reposes,
Waxing well of his deep wound, 1000
In slumber soft, and on the ground
Sadly sits the Assyrian queen;
But far above, in spangled sheen,
Celestial Cupid, her famed son, advanced,
Holds his dear Psyche, sweet entranced 1005
After her wandering labours long,
Till free consent the gods among
Make her his eternal bride,
And from her fair unspotted side
Two blissful twins are to be born, 1010
Youth and Joy; so Jove hath sworn.
    But now my task is smoothly done;
I can fly, or I can run
Quickly to the green earth's end,
Where the bowed welkin slow doth bend, 1015
And from thence can soar as soon
To the corners of the moon.
Mortals, that would follow me,
Love Virtue; she alone is free;
She can teach ye how to climb 1020
Higher than the sphery chime;
Or, if Virtue feeble were,
Heaven itself would stoop to her.

Lycidas

*In this monody the author bewails a learned friend, unfortunately
drowned in his passage from Chester on the Irish Seas, 1637; and,
by occasion, foretells the ruin of our corrupted clergy, then
in their height.*

Yet once more, O ye laurels, and once more
Ye myrtles brown, with ivy never sere,
I come to pluck your berries harsh and crude,

And with forced fingers rude
Shatter your leaves before the mellowing year.   5
Bitter constraint and sad occasion dear
Compels me to disturb your season due;
For Lycidas is dead, dead ere his prime,
Young Lycidas, and hath not left his peer.
Who would not sing for Lycidas? He knew   10
Himself to sing, and build the lofty rhyme.
He must not float upon his watery bier
Unwept, and welter to the parching wind,
Without the meed of some melodious tear.

Begin, then, sisters of the sacred well   15
That from beneath the seat of Jove doth spring;
Begin, and somewhat loudly sweep the string.
Hence with denial vain and coy excuse;
So may some gentle muse
With lucky words favour my destined urn,   20
And as he passes turn,
And bid fair peace be to my sable shroud.

For we were nursed upon the self-same hill,
Fed the same flock, by fountain, shade, and rill;
Together both, ere the high lawns appeared   25
Under the opening eyelids of the morn,
We drove a-field, and both together heard
What time the grey-fly winds her sultry horn,
Battening our flocks with the fresh dews of night,
Oft till the star that rose, at evening, bright,   30
Toward heaven's descent had sloped his westering wheel.
Meanwhile the rural ditties were not mute;
Tempered to the oaten flute,
Rough satyrs danced, and fauns with cloven heel
From the glad sound would not be absent long;   35
And old Damaetus loved to hear our song.

But O the heavy change, now thou art gone,
Now thou art gone and never must return!
Thee, shepherd, thee the woods and desert caves,
With wild thyme and the gadding vine o'ergrown,   40
And all their echoes, mourn.
The willows, and the hazel copses green,
Shall now no more be seen

Fanning their joyous leaves to thy soft lays.
As killing as the canker to the rose,   45
Or taint-worm to the weanling herds that graze,
Or frost to flowers, that their gay wardrobe wear,
When first the white-thorn blows;
Such, Lycidas, thy loss to shepherd's ear.

    Where were ye, nymphs, when the remorseless deep   50
Closed o'er the head of your loved Lycidas?
For neither were ye playing on the steep
Where your old bards, the famous Druids, lie,
Nor on the shaggy top of Mona high,
Nor yet where Deva spreads her wizard stream.   55
Ay me! I fondly dream
'Had ye been there,' . . . for what could that have done?
What could the muse herself that Orpheus bore,
The muse herself, for her enchanting son,
Whom universal nature did lament,   60
When, by the rout that made the hideous roar,
His gory visage down the stream was sent,
Down the swift Hebrus to the Lesbian shore?

    Alas! What boots it with uncessant care
To tend the homely slighted shepherd's trade,   65
And strictly meditate the thankless muse?
Were it not better done, as others use,
To sport with Amaryllis in the shade,
Or with the tangles of Neaera's hair?
Fame is the spur that the clear spirit doth raise   70
(That last infirmity of noble mind)
To scorn delights and live laborious days;
But the fair guerdon when we hope to find,
And think to burst out into sudden blaze,
Comes the blind Fury with the abhorrèd shears,   75
And slits the thin-spun life. 'But not the praise,'
Phoebus replied, and touched my trembling ears:
'Fame is no plant that grows on mortal soil,
Nor in the glistening foil
Set off to the world, nor in broad rumour lies,   80
But lives and spreads aloft by those pure eyes
And perfect witness of all-judging Jove;
As he pronounces lastly on each deed,

Of so much fame in heaven expect thy meed.'
  O fountain Arethuse, and thou honoured flood,   85
Smooth-sliding Mincius, crowned with vocal reeds,
That strain I heard was of a higher mood;
But now my oat proceeds,
And listens to the herald of the sea,
That came in Neptune's plea.   90
He asked the waves, and asked the felon winds,
What hard mishap hath doomed this gentle swain?
And questioned every gust of rugged wings
That blows from off each beakèd promontory:
They knew not of his story;   95
And sage Hippotades their answer brings,
That not a blast was from his dungeon strayed;
The air was calm, and on the level brine
Sleek Panope with all her sisters played.
It was that fatal and perfidious bark,   100
Built in the eclipse, and rigged with curses dark,
That sunk so low that sacred head of thine.
  Next, Camus, reverend sire, went footing slow,
His mantle hairy, and his bonnet sedge,
Inwrought with figures dim, and on the edge   105
Like to that sanguine flower inscribed with woe.
'Ah! who hath reft,' quoth he, 'my dearest pledge?'
Last came, and last did go,
The pilot of the Galilean lake;
Two massy keys he bore of metals twain   110
(The golden opes, the iron shuts amain).
He shook his mitred locks, and stern bespake:
'How well could I have spared for thee, young swain,
Enow of such as, for their bellies' sake,
Creep, and intrude, and climb into the fold!   115
Of other care they little reckoning make
Than how to scramble at the shearers' feast,
And shove away the worthy bidden guest;
Blind mouths! That scarce themselves know how to hold
A sheep-hook, or have learned aught else the least   120
That to the faithful herdman's art belongs!
What recks it them? What need they? They are sped;
And, when they list, their lean and flashy songs

Grate on their scrannel pipes of wretched straw;
The hungry sheep look up, and are not fed,   125
But, swoll'n with wind and the rank mist they draw,
Rot inwardly, and foul contagion spread;
Besides what the grim wolf with privy paw
Daily devours apace, and nothing said.
But that two-handed engine at the door   130
Stands ready to smite once, and smite no more.'
    Return, Alpheus; the dread voice is past
That shrunk thy streams; return Sicilian muse,
And call the vales, and bid them hither cast
Their bells and flowerets of a thousand hues.   135
Ye valleys low, where the mild whispers use
Of shades, and wanton winds, and gushing brooks,
On whose fresh lap the swart star sparely looks,
Throw hither all your quaint enamelled eyes,
That on the green turf suck the honeyed showers,   140
And purple all the ground with vernal flowers.
Bring the rathe primrose that forsaken dies,
The tufted crow-toe, and pale jessamine,
The white pink, and the pansy freaked with jet,
The glowing violet,   145
The musk rose, and the well-attired woodbine,
With cowslips wan that hang the pensive head,
And every flower that sad embroidery wears;
Bid amaranthus all his beauty shed,
And daffadillies fill their cups with tears,   150
To strew the laureate hearse where Lycid lies.
For so, to interpose a little ease,
Let our frail thoughts dally with false surmise.
Ay me! Whilst thee the shores and sounding seas
Wash far away, where'er thy bones are hurled;   155
Whether beyond the stormy Hebrides,
Where thou perhaps under the whelming tide
Visit'st the bottom of the monstrous world;
Or whether thou, to our moist vows denied,
Sleep'st by the fable of Bellerus old,   160
Where the great vision of the guarded mount
Looks toward Namancos and Bayona's hold.

Look homeward, angel, now, and melt with ruth;
And, O ye dolphins, waft the hapless youth.
   Weep no more, woeful shepherds, weep no more,   165
For Lycidas, your sorrow, is not dead,
Sunk though he be beneath the watery floor.
So sinks the day-star in the ocean bed,
And yet anon repairs his drooping head,
And tricks his beams, and with new-spangled ore   170
Flames in the forehead of the morning sky:
So Lycidas sunk low, but mounted high,
Through the dear might of him that walked the waves,
Where, other groves and other streams along,
With nectar pure his oozy locks he laves,   175
And hears the unexpressive nuptial song,
In the blest kingdoms meek of joy and love.
There entertain him all the saints above,
In solemn troops, and sweet societies,
That sing, and singing in their glory move,   180
And wipe the tears for ever from his eyes.
Now, Lycidas, the shepherds weep no more;
Henceforth thou art the genius of the shore,
In thy large recompense, and shalt be good
To all that wander in that perilous flood.   185

   Thus sang the uncouth swain to the oaks and rills,
While the still morn went out with sandals grey;
He touched the tender stops of various quills;
With eager thought warbling his Doric lay:
And now the sun had stretched out all the hills,   190
And now was dropped into the western bay
At last he rose, and twitched his mantle blue:
To-morrow to fresh woods, and pastures new.

Sonnets

I

O nightingale that on yon bloomy spray
  Warblest at eve, when all the woods are still,
  Thou with fresh hope the lover's heart dost fill,
  While the jolly hours lead on propitious May.
Thy liquid notes that close the eye of day,   5
  First heard before the shallow cuckoo's bill,
  Portend success in love. O, if Jove's will
  Have linked that amorous power to thy soft lay,
Now timely sing, ere the rude bird of hate
  Foretell my hopeless doom, in some grove nigh;   10
  As thou from year to year hast sung too late
For my relief, yet hadst no reason why.
  Whether the Muse or Love call thee his mate,
  Both them I serve, and of their train am I.

VII

How soon hath Time, the subtle thief of youth,
  Stolen on his wing my three-and-twentieth year!
  My hasting days fly on with full career,
  But my late spring no bud or blossom showeth.
Perhaps my semblance might deceive the truth,   5
  That I to manhood am arrived so near;
  And inward ripeness doth much less appear,
  That some more timely-happy spirits endueth.
Yet, be it less or more, or soon or slow,
  It shall be still in strictest measure even   10
  To that same lot, however mean or high,
Toward which Time leads me, and the will of heaven,
  All is, if I have grace to use it so,
  As ever in my great task-master's eye.

VIII

WHEN THE ASSAULT WAS INTENDED TO THE CITY

Captain or colonel, or knight in arms,
    Whose chance on these defenceless doors may seize,
    If deed of honour did thee ever please,
    Guard them, and him within protect from harms.
He can requite thee; for he knows the charms   5
    That call fame on such gentle acts as these,
    And he can spread thy name o'er lands and seas,
    Whatever clime the sun's bright circle warms.
Lift not thy spear against the Muses' bower:
    The great Emathian conqueror bid spare   10
    The house of Pindarus, when temple and tower
Went to the ground; and the repeated air
    Of sad Electra's poet had the power
    To save the Athenian walls from ruin bare.

XVIII

ON THE LATE MASSACRE IN PIEDMONT

Avenge, O Lord, thy slaughtered saints, whose bones
    Lie scattered on the Alpine mountains cold;
    Even them who kept thy truth so pure of old,
    When all our fathers worshipped stocks and stones,
Forget not: in thy book record their groans   5
    Who were thy sheep, and in their ancient fold
    Slain by the bloody Piedmontese, that rolled
    Mother with infant down the rocks. Their moans
The vales redoubled to the hills, and they
    To heaven. Their martyred blood and ashes sow   10
    O'er all the Italian fields, where still doth sway
The triple Tyrant; that from these may grow
    A hundredfold, who, having learnt thy way,
    Early may fly the Babylonian woe.

XIX

When I consider how my light is spent
   Ere half my days in this dark world and wide,
   And that one talent which is death to hide
   Lodged with me useless, though my soul more bent
To serve therewith my maker, and present   5
   My true account, lest he returning chide,
   'Doth God exact day-labour, light denied?'
   I fondly ask. But Patience, to prevent
That murmur, soon replies, 'God doth not need
   Either man's work or his own gifts; who best   10
   Bear his mild yoke, they serve him best: his state
Is kingly. Thousands at his bidding speed,
   And post o'er land and ocean without rest;
   They also serve who only stand and wait.'

XXIII

Methought I saw my late espoused saint
   Brought to me like Alcestis from the grave,
   Whom Jove's great son to her glad husband gave,
   Rescued from Death by force, though pale and faint.
Mine, as whom washed from spot of child-bed taint   5
   Purification in the old Law did save,
   And such as yet once more I trust to have
   Full sight of her in heaven without restraint,
Came vested all in white, pure as her mind.
   Her face was veiled; yet to my fancied sight
   Love, sweetness, goodness, in her person shined   10
So clear as in no face with more delight.
   But O as to embrace me she inclined,
   I waked, she fled, and day brought back my night.

Paradise Lost

Book I

Of man's first disobedience, and the fruit
Of that forbidden tree whose mortal taste
Brought death into the world, and all our woe,
With loss of Eden, till one greater man   15
Restore us, and regain the blissful seat,
Sing, heavenly Muse, that, on the secret top
Of Oreb, or of Sinai, didst inspire
That shepherd who first taught the chosen seed
In the beginning how the heavens and earth
Rose out of chaos: or, if Zion hill   10
Delight thee more, and Siloa's brook that flowed
Fast by the oracle of God, I thence
Invoke thy aid to my adventurous song,
That with no middle flight intends to soar
Above the Aonian mount, while it pursues   15
Things unattempted yet in prose or rhyme.
And chiefly thou, O Spirit, that dost prefer
Before all temples the upright heart and pure,
Instruct me, for thou know'st; thou from the first
Wast present, and, with mighty wings outspread, 20
Dove-like sat'st brooding on the vast abyss,
And mad'st it pregnant: what in me is dark
Illumine, what is low raise and support,
That, to the height of this great argument,
I may assert eternal providence,   25
And justify the ways of God to men.
   Say first – for heaven hides nothing from thy view,
Nor the deep tract of hell – say first what cause
Moved our grand parents, in that happy state,
Favoured of heaven so highly, to fall off   30
From their creator, and transgress his will
For one restraint, lords of the world besides.

Who first seduced them to that foul revolt?
     The infernal serpent; he it was whose guile,
Stirred up with envy and revenge, deceived   35
The mother of mankind, what time his pride
Had cast him out from heaven, with all his host
Of rebel angels, by whose aid, aspiring
To set himself in glory above his peers,
He trusted to have equalled the most high,   40
If he opposed, and, with ambitious aim
Against the throne and monarchy of God,
Raised impious war in heaven and battle proud,
With vain attempt. Him the almighty power
Hurled headlong flaming from the ethereal sky,   45
With hideous ruin and combustion, down
To bottomless perdition, there to dwell
In adamantine chains and penal fire,
Who durst defy the omnipotent to arms.
     Nine times the space that measures day and night   50
To mortal men, he with his horrid crew
Lay vanquished, rolling in the fiery gulf,
Confounded, though immortal: but his doom
Reserved him to more wrath; for now the thought
Both of lost happiness and lasting pain   55
Torments him; round he throws his baleful eyes,
That witnessed huge affliction and dismay,
Mixed with obdurate pride and steadfast hate;
At once, as far as angels ken, he views
The dismal situation waste and wild: 60
A dungeon horrible, on all sides round,
As one great furnace flamed, yet from those flames
No light, but rather darkness visible
Served only to discover sights of woe,
Regions of sorrow, doleful shades, where peace   65
And rest can never dwell, hope never comes
That comes to all, but torture without end
Still urges, and a fiery deluge, fed
With ever-burning sulphur unconsumed:
Such place eternal justice had prepared   70
For those rebellious; here their prison ordained
In utter darkness, and their portion set,

As far removed from God and light of heaven
As from the centre thrice to the utmost pole.
O how unlike the place from whence they fell! 75
There the companions of his fall, o'erwhelmed
With floods and whirlwinds of tempestuous fire,
He soon discerns; and weltering by his side,
One next himself in power, and next in crime,
Long after known in Palestine, and named 80
Beëlzebub. To whom the arch-enemy,
And thence in heaven called Satan, with bold words
Breaking the horrid silence, thus began:
  'If thou beest he – but O how fallen! How changed
From him, who in the happy realms of light, 85
Clothed with transcendent brightness, didst outshine
Myriads, though bright – if he whom mutual league,
United thoughts and counsels, equal hope
And hazard in the glorious enterprise,
Joined with me once, now misery hath joined 90
In equal ruin; into what pit thou seest
From what height fallen: so much the stronger proved
He with his thunder: and till then who knew
The force of those dire arms? Yet not for those,
Nor what the potent victor in his rage 95
Can else inflict, do I repent, or change,
Though changed in outward lustre, that fixed mind,
And high disdain from sense of injured merit,
That with the mightiest raised me to contend,
And to the fierce contention brought along 100
Innumerable force of spirits armed,
That durst dislike his reign, and, me preferring,
His utmost power with adverse power opposed
In dubious battle on the plains of heaven,
And shook his throne. What though the field be lost? 105
All is not lost – the unconquerable will,
And study of revenge, immortal hate,
And courage never to submit or yield:
And what is else not to be overcome?
That glory never shall his wrath or might 110
Extort from me. To bow and sue for grace
With suppliant knee, and deify his power

Who, from the terror of this arm, so late
Doubted his empire – that were low indeed;
That were an ignominy and shame beneath   115
This downfall; since, by fate, the strength of gods,
And this empyreal substance, cannot fail;
Since, through experience of this great event,
In arms not worse, in foresight much advanced,
We may with more successful hope resolve   120
To wage by force or guile eternal war,
Irreconcilable to our grand foe,
Who now triumphs, and in the excess of joy
Sole reigning holds the tyranny of heaven.'
     So spake the apostate angel, though in pain,   125
Vaunting aloud, but racked with deep despair;
And him thus answered soon his bold compeer:
     'O Prince, O chief of many thronèd powers
That led the embattled seraphim to war
Under thy conduct, and in dreadful deeds   130
Fearless, endangered heaven's perpetual king,
And put to proof his high supremacy,
Whether upheld by strength, or chance, or fate,
Too well I see and rue the dire event
That, with sad overthrow and foul defeat,   135
Hath lost us heaven, and all this mighty host
In horrible destruction laid thus low,
As far as gods and heavenly essences
Can perish: for the mind and spirit remains
Invincible, and vigour soon returns,   140
Though all our glory extinct, and happy state
Here swallowed up in endless misery.
But what if he our conqueror (whom I now
Of force believe almighty, since no less
Than such could have o'erpowered such force as ours)   145
Have left us this our spirit and strength entire,
Strongly to suffer and support our pains,
That we may so suffice his vengeful ire,
Or do him mightier service as his thralls
By right of war, whate'er his business be,   150
Here in the heart of hell to work in fire,
Or do his errands in the gloomy deep?

What can it then avail though yet we feel
Strength undiminished, or eternal being
To undergo eternal punishment?'   155
    Whereto with speedy words the arch-fiend replied:
'Fallen cherub, to be weak is miserable,
Doing or suffering: but of this be sure –
To do aught good never will be our task,
But ever to do ill our sole delight,   160
As being the contrary to his high will
Whom we resist. If then his providence
Out of our evil seek to bring forth good,
Our labour must be to pervert that end,
And out of good still to find means of evil;   165
Which ofttimes may succeed so as perhaps
Shall grieve him, if I fail not, and disturb
His inmost counsels from their destined aim.
But see, the angry victor hath recalled
His ministers of vengeance and pursuit   170
Back to the gates of heaven: the sulphurous hail,
Shot after us in storm, o'erblown hath laid
The fiery surge that from the precipice
Of heaven received us falling; and the thunder,
Winged with red lightning and impetuous rage,   175
Perhaps hath spent his shafts, and ceases now
To bellow through the vast and boundless deep.
Let us not slip the occasion, whether scorn
Or satiate fury yield it from our foe.
Seest thou yon dreary plain, forlorn and wild,   180
The seat of desolation, void of light,
Save what the glimmering of these livid flames
Casts pale and dreadful? Thither let us tend
From off the tossing of these fiery waves;
There rest, if any rest can harbour there;   185
And, re-assembling our afflicted powers,
Consult how we may henceforth most offend
Our enemy, our own loss how repair,
How overcome this dire calamity,
What reinforcement we may gain from hope,   190
If not, what resolution from despair.'
    Thus Satan, talking to his nearest mate,

With head uplift above the wave, and eyes
That sparkling blazed; his other parts besides
Prone on the flood, extended long and large,   195
Lay floating many a rood, in bulk as huge
As whom the fables name of monstrous size,
Titanian or Earth-born, that warred on Jove,
Briareos or Typhon, whom the den
By ancient Tarsus held, or that sea-beast   200
Leviathan, which God of all his works
Created hugest that swim the ocean stream;
Him, haply slumbering on the Norway foam,
The pilot of some small night-foundered skiff,
Deeming some island, oft, as seamen tell,   205
With fixèd anchor in his scaly rind,
Moors by his side under the lee, while night
Invests the sea, and wishèd morn delays;
So stretched out huge in length the arch-fiend lay,
Chained on the burning lake; nor ever thence   210
Had risen, or heaved his head, but that the will
And high permission of all-ruling heaven
Left him at large to his own dark designs,
That with reiterated crimes he might
Heap on himself damnation, while he sought   215
Evil to others, and enraged might see
How all his malice served but to bring forth
Infinite goodness, grace and mercy, shown
On man by him seduced, but on himself
Treble confusion, wrath, and vengeance poured.   220
   Forthwith upright he rears from off the pool
His mighty stature; on each hand the flames
Driven backward slope their pointing spires, and, rolled
In billows, leave i' the midst a horrid vale.
Then with expanded wings he steers his flight   225
Aloft, incumbent on the dusky air,
That felt unusual weight; till on dry land
He lights – if it were land that ever burned
With solid, as the lake with liquid fire,
And such appeared in hue as when the force   230
Of subterranean wind transports a hill
Torn from Pelorus, or the shattered side

Of thundering Etna, whose combustible
And fuelled entrails, thence conceiving fire,
Sublimed with mineral fury, aid the winds,   235
And leave a singèd bottom all involved
With stench and smoke: such resting found the sole
Of unblessed feet. Him followed his next mate,
Both glorying to have scaped the Stygian flood
As gods, and by their own recovered strength,   240
Not by the sufferance of supernal power.
    'Is this the region, this the soil, the clime,'
Said then the lost archangel, 'this the seat
That we must change for heaven, this mournful gloom
For that celestial light? Be it so, since he   245
Who now is sovereign can dispose and bid
What shall be right; farthest from him is best,
Whom reason hath equalled, force hath made supreme
Above his equals. Farewell, happy fields,
Where joy for ever dwells; hail, horrors, hail,   250
Infernal world; and thou, profoundest hell,
Receive thy new possessor – one who brings
A mind not to be changed by place or time.
The mind is its own place, and in itself
Can make a heaven of hell, a hell of heaven.   255
What matter where, if I be still the same,
And what I should be, all, but less than he
Whom thunder hath made greater? Here at least
We shall be free; the almighty hath not built
Here for his envy, will not drive us hence: 260
Here we may reign secure; and, in my choice,
To reign is worth ambition, though in hell:
Better to reign in hell than serve in heaven.
But wherefore let we then our faithful friends,
The associates and co-partners of our loss,   265
Lie thus astonished on the oblivious pool,
And call them not to share with us their part
In this unhappy mansion, or once more
With rallied arms to try what may be yet
Regained in heaven, or what more lost in hell?'   270
    So Satan spake, and him Beëlzebub
Thus answered: 'Leader of those armies bright

Which, but the omnipotent, none could have foiled;
If once they hear that voice, their liveliest pledge
Of hope in fears and dangers – heard so oft   275
In worst extremes, and on the perilous edge
Of battle, when it raged, in all assaults
Their surest signal – they will soon resume
New courage and revive, though now they lie
Grovelling and prostrate on yon lake of fire,   280
As we erewhile, astounded and amazed;
No wonder, fallen such a pernicious height.'
       He scarce had ceased when the superior fiend
Was moving toward the shore; his ponderous shield,
Ethereal temper, massy, large, and round,   285
Behind him cast; the broad circumference
Hung on his shoulders like the moon, whose orb
Through optic glass the Tuscan artist views
At evening, from the top of Fesolè,
Or in Valdarno, to descry new lands,   290
Rivers, or mountains, in her spotty globe.
His spear – to equal which the tallest pine
Hewn on Norwegian hills, to be the mast
Of some great ammiral, were but a wand –
He walked with, to support uneasy steps   295
Over the burning marl, not like those steps
On heaven's azure; and the torrid clime
Smote on him sore besides, vaulted with fire;
Nathless he so endured, till on the beach
Of that inflamèd sea he stood, and called   300
His legions – angel forms, who lay entranced
Thick as autumnal leaves that strew the brooks
In Vallombrosa, where the Etrurian shades
High over-arched embower; or scattered sedge
Afloat, when with fierce winds Orion armed   305
Hath vexed the Red Sea coast, whose waves o'erthrew
Busiris and his Memphian chivalry,
While with perfidious hatred they pursued
The sojourners of Goshen, who beheld
From the safe shore their floating carcasses   310
And broken chariot-wheels: so thick bestrewn,
Abject and lost, lay these, covering the flood,

Under amazement of their hideous change.
He called so loud that all the hollow deep
Of hell resounded: 'Princes, potentates,   315
Warriors, the flower of heaven – once yours; now lost,
If such astonishment as this can seize
Eternal spirits; or have ye chosen this place
After the toil of battle to repose
Your wearied virtue, for the ease you find   320
To slumber here, as in the vales of heaven?
Or in this abject posture have ye sworn
To adore the conqueror, who now beholds
Cherub and seraph rolling in the flood
With scattered arms and ensigns, till anon   325
His swift pursuers from heaven-gates discern
The advantage, and, descending, tread us down
Thus drooping, or with linkèd thunderbolts
Transfix us to the bottom of this gulf?
Awake, arise, or be for ever fallen.'   330
    They heard, and were abashed, and up they sprung
Upon the wing, as when men wont to watch,
On duty sleeping found by whom they dread,
Rouse and bestir themselves ere well awake.
Nor did they not perceive the evil plight   335
In which they were, or the fierce pains not feel;
Yet to their general's voice they soon obeyed
Innumerable. As when the potent rod
Of Amram's son, in Egypt's evil day,
Waved round the coast, up called a pitchy cloud   340
Of locusts, warping on the eastern wind,
That o'er the realm of impious Pharaoh hung
Like night, and darkened all the land of Nile;
So numberless were those bad angels seen
Hovering on wing under the cope of hell,   345
'Twixt upper, nether, and surrounding fires;
Till, as a signal given, the uplifted spear
Of their great sultan waving to direct
Their course, in even balance down they light
On the firm brimstone, and fill all the plain: 350
A multitude like which the populous North
Poured never from her frozen loins to pass

Rhene or the Danaw, when her barbarous sons
Came like a deluge on the South, and spread
Beneath Gibraltar to the Libyan sands.   355
Forthwith, from every squadron and each band,
The heads and leaders thither haste where stood
Their great commander – godlike shapes, and forms
Excelling human, princely dignities,
And powers that erst in heaven sat on thrones;   360
Though of their names in heavenly records now
Be no memorial, blotted out and razed
By their rebellion from the Books of Life.
Nor had they yet among the sons of Eve
Got them new names, till wandering o'er the earth,   365
Through God's high sufferance for the trial of man,
By falsities and lies the greatest part
Of mankind they corrupted to forsake
God their creator, and the invisible
Glory of him that made them, to transform   370
Oft to the image of a brute, adorned
With gay religions full of pomp and gold,
And devils to adore for deities:
Then were they known to men by various names,
And various idols through the heathen world.   375
   Say, Muse, their names then known, who first, who last,
Roused from the slumber on that fiery couch,
At their great emperor's call, as next in worth
Came singly where he stood on the bare strand,
While the promiscuous crowd stood yet aloof.   380
   The chief were those who, from the pit of hell
Roaming to seek their prey on earth, durst fix
Their seats, long after, next the seat of God,
Their altars by his altar, gods adored
Among the nations round, and durst abide   385
Jehovah thundering out of Zion, throned
Between the cherubim; yea, often placed
Within his sanctuary itself their shrines,
Abominations; and with cursed things
His holy rites and solemn feasts profaned,   390
And with their darkness durst affront his light.
First, Moloch, horrid king, besmeared with blood

Of human sacrifice, and parents' tears;
Though for the noise of drums and timbrels loud,
Their children's cries unheard that passed through fire   395
To his grim idol. Him the Ammonite
Worshipped in Rabba and her watery plain,
In Argob and in Basan, to the stream
Of utmost Arnon. Nor content with such
Audacious neighbourhooood, the wisest heart   400
Of Solomon he led by fraud to build
His temple right against the temple of God
On that opprobrious hill, and made his grove
The pleasant valley of Hinnom, Tophet thence
And black Gehenna called, the type of hell.   405
Next Chemos, the obscene dread of Moab's sons,
From Aroer to Nebo and the wild
Of southmost Abarim; in Hesebon
And Horonaim, Seon's realm, beyond
The flowery dale of Sibma clad with vines,   410
And Elealè to the Asphaltic Pool:
Peor his other name, when he enticed
Israel in Sittim, on their march from Nile,
To do him wanton rites, which cost them woe.
Yet thence his lustful orgies he enlarged   415
Even to that hill of scandal, by the grove
Of Moloch homicide, lust hard by hate,
Till good Josiah drove them thence to hell.
With these came they who, from the bordering flood
Of old Euphrates to the brook that parts   420
Egypt from Syrian ground, had general names
Of Baälim and Ashtaroth – those male,
These feminine. For spirits, when they please,
Can either sex assume, or both; so soft
And uncompounded is their essence pure,   425
Not tied or manacled with joint or limb,
Nor founded on the brittle strength of bones,
Like cumbrous flesh; but in what shape they choose,
Dilated or condensed, bright or obscure,
Can execute their airy purposes,   430
And works of love or enmity fulfil.
For those the race of Israel oft forsook

Their living strength, and unfrequented left
His righteous altar, bowing lowly down
To bestial gods; for which their heads, as low   435
Bowed down in battle, sunk before the spear
Of despicable foes. With these in troop
Came Ashtoreth, whom the Phoenicians called
Astarte, queen of heaven, with crescent horns;
To whose bright image nightly by the moon   440
Sidonian virgins paid their vows and songs;
In Zion also not unsung, where stood
Her temple on the offensive mountain, built
By that uxorious king whose heart, though large,
Beguiled by fair idolatresses, fell   445
To idols foul. Thammuz came next behind,
Whose annual wound in Lebanon allured
The Syrian damsels to lament his fate
In amorous ditties all a summer's day,
While smooth Adonis from his native rock   450
Ran purple to the sea, supposed with blood
Of Thammuz yearly wounded; the love-tale
Infected Zion's daughters with like heat,
Whose wanton passions in the sacred porch
Ezekiel saw, when by the vision led   455
His eye surveyed the dark idolatries
Of alienated Judah. Next came one
Who mourned in earnest, when the captive ark
Maimed his brute image, head and hands lopped off,
In his own temple, on the groundsel edge,   460
Where he fell flat and shamed his worshippers:
Dagon his name, sea-monster, upward man
And downward fish; yet had his temple high
Reared in Azotus, dreaded through the coast
Of Palestine, in Gath and Ascalon,   465
And Accaron and Gaza's frontier bounds.
Him followed Rimmon, whose delightful seat
Was fair Damascus, on the fertile banks
Of Abbana and Pharphar, lucid streams.
He also against the house of God was bold: 470
A leper once he lost, and gained a king –
Ahaz, his sottish conqueror, whom he drew

God's altar to disparage and displace
For one of Syrian mode, whereon to burn
His odious offerings, and adore the gods 475
Whom he had vanquished. After these appeared
A crew who, under names of old renown –
Osiris, Isis, Orus, and their train –
With monstrous shapes and sorceries abused
Fanatic Egypt and her priests to seek 480
Their wandering gods disguised in brutish forms
Rather than human. Nor did Israel scape
The infection, when their borrowed gold composed
The calf in Oreb; and the rebel king
Doubled that sin in Bethel and in Dan, 485
Likening his maker to the grazèd ox –
Jehovah, who, in one night, when he passed
From Egypt marching, equalled with one stroke
Both her first-born and all her bleating gods.
Belial came last; than whom a spirit more lewd 490
Fell not from heaven, or more gross to love
Vice for itself: to him no temple stood
Or altar smoked; yet who more oft than he
In temples and at altars, when the priest
Turns atheist, as did Eli's sons, who filled 495
With lust and violence the house of God?
In courts and palaces he also reigns,
And in luxurious cities, where the noise
Of riot ascends above their loftiest towers,
And injury and outrage; and when night 500
Darkens the streets, then wander forth the sons
Of Belial, flown with insolence and wine.
Witness the streets of Sodom, and that night
In Gibeah, when the hospitable door
Exposed a matron, to avoid worse rape. 505
  These were the prime in order and in might:
The rest were long to tell, though far renowned,
The Ionian gods – of Javan's issue held
Gods, yet confessed later than heaven and earth,
Their boasted parents – Titan, heaven's first-born, 510
With his enormous brood, and birthright seized
By younger Saturn: he from mightier Jove,

His own and Rhea's son, like measure found;
So Jove usurping reigned; these, first in Crete
And Ida known, thence on the snowy top   515
Of cold Olympus ruled the middle air,
Their highest heaven; or on the Delphian cliff,
Or in Dodona, and through all the bounds
Of Doric land; or who with Saturn old
Fled over Adria to the Hesperian fields,   520
And o'er the Celtic roamed the utmost isles.

   All these and more came flocking; but with looks
Downcast and damp; yet such wherein appeared
Obscure some glimpse of joy to have found their chief
Not in despair, to have found themselves not lost   525
In loss itself; which on his countenance cast
Like doubtful hue; but he, his wonted pride
Soon recollecting, with high words, that bore
Semblance of worth, not substance, gently raised
Their fainting courage, and dispelled their fears.   530
Then straight commands that, at the warlike sound
Of trumpets loud and clarions, be upreared
His mighty standard; that proud honour claimed
Azazel as his right, a cherub tall:
Who forthwith from the glittering staff unfurled   535
The imperial ensign, which, full high advanced,
Shone like a meteor streaming to the wind,
With gems and golden lustre rich emblazed,
Seraphic arms and trophies; all the while
Sonorous metal blowing martial sounds: 540
At which the universal host upsent
A shout that tore hell's concave, and beyond
Frighted the reign of Chaos and old Night.
All in a moment through the gloom were seen
Ten thousand banners rise into the air,   545
With orient colours waving: with them rose
A forest huge of spears; and thronging helms
Appeared, and serried shields in thick array
Of depth immeasurable; anon they move
In perfect phalanx to the Dorian mood   550
Of flutes and soft recorders – such as raised
To height of noblest temper heroes old

Arming to battle, and instead of rage
Deliberate valour breathed, firm and unmoved
With dread of death to flight or foul retreat;   555
Nor wanting power to mitigate and swage
With solemn touches troubled thoughts, and chase
Anguish and doubt and fear and sorrow and pain
From mortal or immortal minds. Thus they,
Breathing united force with fixèd thought,   560
Moved on in silence to soft pipes that charmed
Their painful steps o'er the burnt soil; and now
Advanced in view they stand – a horrid front
Of dreadful length and dazzling arms, in guise
Of warriors old, with ordered spear and shield,   565
Awaiting what command their mighty chief
Had to impose: he through the armèd files
Darts his experienced eye, and soon traverse
The whole battalion views – their order due,
Their visages and stature as of gods;   570
Their number last he sums. And now his heart
Distends with pride, and, hardening in his strength,
Glories: for never, since created man,
Met such embodied force as, named with these,
Could merit more than that small infantry   575
Warred on by cranes – though all the giant brood
Of Phlegra with the heroic race were joined
That fought at Thebes and Ilium, on each side
Mixed with auxiliar gods; and what resounds
In fable or romance of Uther's son,   580
Begirt with British and Armoric knights;
And all who since, baptized or infidel,
Jousted in Aspramont, or Montalban,
Damasco, or Marocco, or Trebizond,
Or whom Bizerta sent from Afric shore   585
When Charlemagne with all his peerage fell
By Fontarabbia. Thus far these beyond
Compare of mortal prowess, yet observed
Their dread commander; he above the rest
In shape and gesture proudly eminent,   590
Stood like a tower; his form had yet not lost
All her original brightness, nor appeared

Less than archangel ruined, and the excess
Of glory obscured: as when the sun new risen
Looks through the horizontal misty air   595
Shorn of his beams, or from behind the moon
In dim eclipse, disastrous twilight sheds
On half the nations, and with fear of change
Perplexes monarchs. Darkened so, yet shone
Above them all the archangel: but his face   600
Deep scars of thunder had intrenched, and care
Sat on his faded cheek, but under brows
Of dauntless courage, and considerate pride
Waiting revenge; cruel his eye, but cast
Signs of remorse and passion, to behold   605
The fellows of his crime, the followers rather
(Far other once beheld in bliss), condemned
For ever now to have their lot in pain –
Millions of spirits for his fault amerced
Of heaven, and from eternal splendours flung   610
For his revolt – yet faithful how they stood,
Their glory withered; as, when heaven's fire
Hath scathed the forest oaks or mountain pines,
With singèd top their stately growth, though bare,
Stands on the blasted heath. He now prepared   615
To speak; whereat their doubled ranks they bend
From wing to wing, and half enclose him round
With all his peers: attention held them mute.
Thrice he assayed, and thrice, in spite of scorn,
Tears, such as angels weep, burst forth: at last   620
Words interwove with sighs found out their way:
   'O myriads of immortal spirits, O powers
Matchless, but with the Almighty – and that strife
Was not inglorious, though the event was dire,
As this place testifies, and this dire change,   625
Hateful to utter; but what power of mind,
Foreseeing or presaging, from the depth
Of knowledge past or present, could have feared
How such united force of gods, how such
As stood like these, could ever know repulse?   630
For who can yet believe, though after loss,
That all these puissant legions, whose exile

Hath emptied heaven, shall fail to re-ascend,
Self-raised, and repossess their native seat?
For me be witness all the host of heaven   635
If counsels different, or danger shunned
By me, have lost our hopes. But he who reigns
Monarch in heaven, till then as one secure
Sat on his throne, upheld by old repute,
Consent or custom, and his regal state   640
Put forth at full, but still his strength concealed –
Which tempted our attempt, and wrought our fall.
Henceforth his might we know, and know our own,
So as not either to provoke, or dread
New war provoked: our better part remains   645
To work in close design, by fraud or guile,
What force effected not; that he no less
At length from us may find, who overcomes
By force hath overcome but half his foe.
Space may produce new worlds; whereof so rife   650
There went a fame in heaven that he ere long
Intended to create, and therein plant
A generation whom his choice regard
Should favour equal to the sons of heaven.
Thither, if but to pry, shall be perhaps   655
Our first eruption – thither, or elsewhere;
For this infernal pit shall never hold
Celestial spirits in bondage, nor the abyss
Long under darkness cover. But these thoughts
Full counsel must mature; peace is despaired,   660
For who can think submission? War, then, war
Open or understood, must be resolved.'
    He spake; and to confirm his words, outflew
Millions of flaming swords, drawn from the thighs
Of mighty cherubim; the sudden blaze   665
Far round illumined hell; highly they raged
Against the highest, and fierce with graspèd arms
Clashed on their sounding shields the din of war,
Hurling defiance toward the vault of heaven.
    There stood a hill not far, whose grisly top   670
Belched fire and rolling smoke; the rest entire
Shone with a glossy scurf – undoubted sign

That in his womb was hid metallic ore,
The work of sulphur. Thither, winged with speed,
A numerous brigade hastened: as when bands   675
Of pioneers with spade and pickaxe armed,
Forerun the royal camp, to trench a field,
Or cast a rampart. Mammon led them on –
Mammon, the least erected spirit that fell
From heaven; for even in heaven his looks and thoughts   680
Were always downward bent, admiring more
The riches of heaven's pavement, trodden gold,
Than aught divine or holy else enjoyed
In vision beatific; by him first
Men also, and by his suggestion taught,   685
Ransacked the centre, and with impious hands
Rifled the bowels of their mother earth
For treasures better hid. Soon had his crew
Opened into the hill a spacious wound,
And digged out ribs of gold. Let none admire   690
That riches grow in hell; that soil may best
Deserve the precious bane. And here let those
Who boast in mortal things, and wondering tell
Of Babel, and the works of Memphian kings.
Learn how their greatest monuments of fame   695
And strength, and art, are easily outdone
By spirits reprobate, and in an hour
What in an age they, with incessant toil
And hands innumerable, scarce perform.
Nigh on the plain, in many cells prepared,   700
That underneath had veins of liquid fire
Sluiced from the lake, a second multitude
With wondrous art founded the massy ore,
Severing each kind, and scummed the bullion-dross.
A third as soon had formed within the ground   705
A various mould, and from the boiling cells
By strange conveyance filled each hollow nook;
As in an organ, from one blast of wind,
To many a row of pipes the sound-board breathes.
Anon out of the earth a fabric huge   710
Rose like an exhalation, with the sound
Of dulcet symphonies and voices sweet –

Built like a temple, where pilasters round
Were set, and Doric pillars overlaid
With golden architrave; nor did there want   715
Cornice or frieze, with bossy sculptures graven;
The roof was fretted gold. Not Babylon
Nor great Alcairo such magnificence
Equalled in all their glories, to enshrine
Belus or Serapis their gods, or seat   720
Their kings, when Egypt with Assyria strove
In wealth and luxury. The ascending pile
Stood fixed her stately height; and straight the doors,
Opening their brazen folds discover, wide
Within, her ample spaces o'er the smooth   725
And level pavement: from the archèd roof,
Pendent by subtle magic, many a row
Of starry lamps and blazing cressets, fed
With naphtha and asphaltus, yielded light
As from a sky. The hasty multitude   730
Admiring entered; and the work some praise,
And some the architect: his hand was known
In heaven by many a towered structure high,
Where sceptred angels held their residence,
And sat as princes, whom the supreme king   735
Exalted to such power, and gave to rule,
Each in his hierarchy, the orders bright.
Nor was his name unheard or unadored
In ancient Greece; and in Ausonian land
Men called him Mulciber; and how he fell   740
From heaven they fabled, thrown by angry Jove
Sheer o'er the crystal battlements: from morn
To noon he fell, from noon to dewy eve,
A summer's day, and with the setting sun
Dropped from the zenith, like a falling star,   745
On Lemnos, the Aegean isle: thus they relate,
Erring; for he with his rebellious rout
Fell long before; nor aught availed him now
To have built in heaven high towers; nor did he scape
By all his engines, but was headlong sent,   750
With his industrious crew, to build in hell.
    Meanwhile the wingèd heralds, by command

Of sovereign power, with awful ceremony
And trumpet's sound, throughout the host proclaim
A solemn council forthwith to be held   755
At Pandemonium, the high capital
Of Satan and his peers; their summons called
From every band and squarèd regiment
By place or choice the worthiest; they anon
With hundreds and with thousands trooping came   760
Attended; all access was thronged; the gates
And porches wide, but chief the spacious hall
(Though like a covered field, where champions bold
Wont ride in armed, and at the soldan's chair
Defied the best of paynim chivalry   765
To mortal combat, or career with lance),
Thick swarmed, both on the ground and in the air,
Brushed with the hiss of rustling wings. As bees
In spring-time, when the sun with Taurus rides,
Pour forth their populous youth about the hive   770
In clusters; they among fresh dews and flowers
Fly to and fro, or on the smoothèd plank,
The suburb of their straw-built citadel,
New rubbed with balm, expatiate, and confer
Their state-affairs: so thick the airy crowd   775
Swarmed and were straitened; till, the signal given
Behold a wonder! They but now who seemed
In bigness to surpass Earth's giant sons,
Now less than smallest dwarfs, in narrow room
Throng numberless – like that pygmean race   780
Beyond the Indian mount, or fairy elves,
Whose midnight revels, by a forest side
Or fountain, some belated peasant sees,
Or dreams he sees, while overhead the moon
Sits arbitress, and nearer to the earth   785
Wheels her pale course: they, on their mirth and dance
Intent, with jocund music charm his ear;
At once with joy and fear his heart rebounds.
Thus incorporeal spirits to smallest forms
Reduced their shapes immense, and were at large,   790
Though without number still amidst the hall
Of that infernal court. But far within,

And in their own dimensions like themselves,
The great seraphic lords and cherubim
In close recess and secret conclave sat,   795
A thousand demi-gods on golden seats,
Frequent and full. After short silence then,
And summons read, the great consult began.

THE END OF THE FIRST BOOK

Book II

High on a throne of royal state, which far
Outshone the wealth of Ormus and of Ind,
Or where the gorgeous East with richest hand
Showers on her kings barbaric pearl and gold,
Satan exalted sat, by merit raised   5
To that bad eminence; and, from despair
Thus high uplifted beyond hope, aspires
Beyond thus high, insatiate to pursue
Vain war with heaven; and, by success untaught,
His proud imaginations thus displayed: 10
    'Powers and dominions, deities of heaven –
For since no deep within her gulf can hold
Immortal vigour, though oppressed and fallen,
I give not heaven for lost. From this descent
Celestial virtues rising will appear   15
More glorious and more dread than from no fall,
And trust themselves to fear no second fate –
Me though just right, and the fixed laws of heaven,
Did first create your leader – next, free choice,
With what besides in council or in fight   20
Hath been achieved of merit – yet this loss,
Thus far at least recovered, hath much more
Established in a safe unenvied throne,
Yielded with full consent. The happier state
In heaven, which follows dignity, might draw   25
Envy from each inferior; but who here

Will envy whom the highest place exposes
Foremost to stand against the thunderer's aim
Your bulwark, and condemns to greatest share
Of endless pain? Where there is, then, no good   30
For which to strive, no strife can grow up there
From faction: for none sure will claim in hell
Precedence; none whose portion is so small
Of present pain that with ambitious mind
Will covet more. With this advantage, then,   35
To union, and firm faith, and firm accord,
More than can be in heaven, we now return
To claim our just inheritance of old,
Surer to prosper than prosperity
Could have assured us; and by what best way,   40
Whether of open war or covert guile,
We now debate: who can advise may speak.'
    He ceased; and next him Moloch, sceptred king,
Stood up – the strongest and the fiercest spirit
That fought in heaven, now fiercer by despair.   45
His trust was with the eternal to be deemed
Equal in strength, and rather than be less
Cared not to be at all; with that care lost
Went all his fear: of God, or hell, or worse,
He recked not, and these words thereafter spake: 50
    'My sentence is for open war; of wiles,
More unexpert, I boast not: them let those
Contrive who need, or when they need; not now.
For while they sit contriving, shall the rest –
Millions that stand in arms, and longing wait   55
The signal to ascend – sit lingering here,
Heaven's fugitives, and for their dwelling place
Accept this dark opprobrious den of shame,
The prison of his tyranny who reigns
By our delay? No, let us rather choose,   60
Armed with hell flames and fury all at once
O'er heaven's high towers to force resistless way,
Turning our tortures into horrid arms
Against the torturer; when to meet the noise
Of his almighty engine, he shall hear   65
Infernal thunder, and for lightning see

Black fire and horror shot with equal rage
Among his angels, and his throne itself
Mixed with Tartarean sulphur and strange fire,
His own invented torments. But perhaps 70
The way seems difficult, and steep to scale
With upright wing against a higher foe.
Let such bethink them, if the sleepy drench
Of that forgetful lake benumb not still,
That in our proper motion we ascend 75
Up to our native seat; descent and fall
To us is adverse. Who but felt of late,
When the fierce foe hung on our broken rear
Insulting, and pursued us through the deep,
With what compulsion and laborious flight 80
We sunk thus low? The ascent is easy, then;
The event is feared; should we again provoke
Our stronger, some worse way his wrath may find
To our destruction, if there be in hell
Fear to be worse destroyed; what can be worse 85
Than to dwell here, driven out from bliss, condemned
In this abhorrèd deep to utter woe;
Where pain of unextinguishable fire
Must exercise us without hope of end
The vassals of his anger, when the scourge 90
Inexorably, and the torturing hour,
Calls us to penance? More destroyed than thus,
We should be quite abolished, and expire.
What fear we then? What doubt we to incense
His utmost ire? Which, to the height enraged, 95
Will either quite consume us, and reduce
To nothing this essential – happier far
Than miserable to have eternal being –
Or, if our substance be indeed divine,
And cannot cease to be, we are at worst 100
On this side nothing; and by proof we feel
Our power sufficient to disturb his heaven,
And with perpetual inroads to alarm,
Though inaccessible, his fatal throne:
Which, if not victory, is yet revenge.' 105
  He ended frowning, and his look denounced

Desperate revenge, and battle dangerous
To less than gods. On the other side up rose
Belial, in act more graceful and humane;
A fairer person lost not heaven; he seemed   110
For dignity composed, and high exploit:
But all was false and hollow; though his tongue
Dropped manna, and could make the worse appear
The better reason, to perplex and dash
Maturest counsels: for his thoughts were low –   115
To vice industrious, but to nobler deeds
Timorous and slothful; yet he pleased the ear,
And with persuasive accent thus began:
    'I should be much for open war, O peers,
As not behind in hate, if what was urged   120
Main reason to persuade immediate war
Did not dissuade me most, and seem to cast
Ominous conjecture on the whole success;
When he who most excels in fact of arms,
In what he counsels and in what excels   125
Mistrustful, grounds his courage on despair
And utter dissolution, as the scope
Of all his aim, after some dire revenge.
First, what revenge? The towers of heaven are filled
With armèd watch, that render all access   130
Impregnable: oft on the bordering deep
Encamp their legions, or with obscure wing
Scout far and wide into the realm of night,
Scorning surprise. Or could we break our way
By force, and at our heels all hell should rise   135
With blackest insurrection to confound
Heaven's purest light, yet our great enemy,
All incorruptible, would on his throne
Sit unpolluted, and the ethereal mould,
Incapable of stain, would soon expel   140
Her mischief, and purge off the baser fire,
Victorious. Thus repulsed, our final hope
Is flat despair: we must exasperate
The almighty victor to spend all his rage,
And that must end us, that must be our cure –   145
To be no more; sad cure; for who would lose,

Though full of pain, this intellectual being,
Those thoughts that wander through eternity,
To perish rather, swallowed up and lost
In the wide womb of uncreated night,   150
Devoid of sense and motion? And who knows,
Let this be good, whether our angry foe
Can give it, or will ever? How he can
Is doubtful; that he never will is sure.
Will he, so wise, let loose at once his ire,   155
Belike through impotence or unaware,
To give his enemies their wish, and end
Them in his anger whom his anger saves
To punish endless? "Wherefore cease we, then?"
Say they who counsel war; "we are decreed,   160
Reserved, and destined to eternal woe;
Whatever doing, what can we suffer more,
What can we suffer worse?" Is this, then, worst –
Thus sitting, thus consulting, thus in arms?
What when we fled amain, pursued and struck   165
With heaven's afflicting thunder, and besought
The deep to shelter us? This hell then seemed
A refuge from those wounds; or when we lay
Chained on the burning lake? That sure was worse.
What if the breath that kindled those grim fires,   170
Awaked, should blow them into sevenfold rage,
And plunge us in the flames? Or from above
Should intermitted vengeance arm again
His red right hand to plague us? What if all
Her stores were opened, and this firmament   175
Of hell should spout her cataracts of fire,
Impendent horrors, threatening hideous fall
One day upon our heads; while we perhaps,
Designing or exhorting glorious war,
Caught in a fiery tempest, shall be hurled,   180
Each on his rock transfixed, the sport and prey
Of racking whirlwinds, or for ever sunk
Under yon boiling ocean, wrapped in chains,
There to converse with everlasting groans,
Unrespited, unpitied, unreprieved,   185
Ages of hopeless end? This would be worse.

War, therefore, open or concealed, alike
My voice dissuades; for what can force or guile
With him, or who deceive his mind, whose eye
Views all things at one view? He from heaven's height   190
All these our motions vain sees and derides,
Not more almighty to resist our might
Than wise to frustrate all our plots and wiles.
Shall we, then, live thus vile – the race of heaven
Thus trampled, thus expelled, to suffer here   195
Chains and these torments? Better these than worse,
By my advice; since fate inevitable
Subdues us, and omnipotent decree,
The victor's will. To suffer, as to do,
Our strength is equal, nor the law unjust   200
That so ordains; this was at first resolved,
If we were wise, against so great a foe
Contending, and so doubtful what might fall.
I laugh when those who at the spear are bold
And venturous, if that fail them, shrink, and fear   205
What yet they know must follow – to endure
Exile, or ignominy, or bonds, or pain,
The sentence of their conqueror: this is now
Our doom; which if we can sustain and bear,
Our supreme foe in time may much remit   210
His anger, and perhaps, thus far removed,
Not mind us not offending, satisfied
With what is punished; whence these raging fires
Will slacken, if his breath stir not their flames.
Our purer essence then will overcome   215
Their noxious vapour, or, inured, not feel,
Or, changed at length, and to the place conformed
In temper and in nature, will receive
Familiar the fierce heat; and, void of pain,
This horror will grow mild, this darkness light;   220
Besides what hope the never-ending flight
Of future days may bring, what chance, what change
Worth waiting – since our present lot appears
For happy though but ill, for ill not worst,
If we procure not to ourselves more woe.'   225
    Thus Belial, with words clothed in reason's garb,

Counselled ignoble ease and peaceful sloth,
Not peace; and after him thus Mammon spake:
   'Either to disenthrone the king of heaven
We war, if war be best, or to regain   230
Our own right lost; him to unthrone we then
May hope, when everlasting Fate shall yield
To fickle Chance, and Chaos judge the strife:
The former, vain to hope, argues as vain
The latter; for what place can be for us   235
Within heaven's bound, unless heaven's lord supreme
We overpower? Suppose he should relent,
And publish grace to all, on promise made
Of new subjection; with what eyes could we
Stand in his presence humble, and receive   240
Strict laws imposed, to celebrate his throne
With warbled hymns, and to his Godhead sing
Forced halleluiahs, while he lordly sits
Our envied sovereign, and his altar breathes
Ambrosial odours and ambrosial flowers,   245
Our servile offerings? This must be our task
In heaven, this our delight; how wearisome
Eternity so spent in worship paid
To whom we hate. Let us not then pursue,
By force impossible, by leave obtained   250
Unacceptable, though in heaven, our state
Of splendid vassalage; but rather seek
Our own good from ourselves, and from our own
Live to ourselves, though in this vast recess,
Free and to none accountable, preferring   255
Hard liberty before the easy yoke
Of servile pomp. Our greatness will appear
Then most conspicuous when great things of small,
Useful of hurtful, prosperous of adverse,
We can create, and in what place so e'er   260
Thrive under evil, and work ease out of pain
Through labour and endurance. This deep world
Of darkness do we dread? How oft amidst
Thick clouds and dark doth heaven's all-ruling sire
Choose to reside, his glory unobscured,   265
And with the majesty of darkness round

Covers his throne, from whence deep thunders roar,
Mustering their rage, and heaven resembles hell?
As he our darkness, cannot we his light
Imitate when we please? This desert soil   270
Wants not her hidden lustre, gems and gold;
Nor want we skill or art from whence to raise
Magnificence; and what can heaven show more?
Our torments also may, in length of time,
Become our elements, these piercing fires   275
As soft as now severe, our temper changed
Into their temper; which must needs remove
The sensible of pain. All things invite
To peaceful counsels, and the settled state
Of order, how in safety best we may   280
Compose our present evils, with regard
Of what we are and where, dismissing quite
All thoughts of war; ye have what I advise.'
   He scarce had finished, when such murmur filled
The assembly as when hollow rocks retain   285
The sound of blustering winds, which all night long
Had roused the sea, now with hoarse cadence lull
Seafaring men o'erwatched, whose bark by chance,
Or pinnace, anchors in a craggy bay
After the tempest; such applause was heard   290
As Mammon ended, and his sentence pleased,
Advising peace: for such another field
They dreaded worse than hell; so much the fear
Of thunder and the sword of Michaël
Wrought still within them; and no less desire   295
To found this nether empire, which might rise,
By policy and long process of time,
In emulation opposite to heaven.
Which when Beëlzebub perceived – than whom,
Satan except, none higher sat – with grave   300
Aspect he rose, and in his rising seemed
A pillar of state; deep on his front engraven
Deliberation sat, and public care;
And princely counsel in his face yet shone,
Majestic, though in ruin; sage he stood,   305
With Atlantean shoulders, fit to bear

The weight of mightiest monarchies; his look
Drew audience and attention still as night
Or summer's noontide air, while thus he spake:
   'Thrones and imperial powers, offspring of heaven;   310
Ethereal virtues; or these titles now
Must we renounce, and, changing style, be called
Princes of hell? For so the popular vote
Inclines – here to continue, and build up here
A growing empire; doubtless; while we dream,   315
And know not that the king of heaven hath doomed
This place our dungeon – not our safe retreat
Beyond his potent arm, to live exempt
From heaven's high jurisdiction, in new league
Banded against his throne, but to remain   320
In strictest bondage, though thus far removed,
Under the inevitable curb, reserved
His captive multitude; for he, be sure,
In height or depth, still first and last will reign
Sole king, and of his kingdom lose no part   325
By our revolt, but over hell extend
His empire, and with iron sceptre rule
Us here, as with his golden those in heaven.
What sit we then projecting peace and war?
War hath determined us, and foiled with loss   330
Irreparable; terms of peace yet none
Vouchsafed or sought; for what peace will be given
To us enslaved, but custody severe,
And stripes and arbitrary punishment
Inflicted? And what peace can we return,   335
But, to our power, hostility and hate,
Untamed reluctance, and revenge, though slow,
Yet ever plotting how the conqueror least
May reap his conquest, and may least rejoice
In doing what we most in suffering feel?   340
Nor will occasion want, nor shall we need
With dangerous expedition to invade
Heaven, whose high walls fear no assault or siege,
Or ambush from the deep. What if we find
Some easier enterprise? There is a place   345
(If ancient and prophetic fame in heaven

Err not) – another world, the happy seat
Of some new race called Man, about this time
To be created like to us, though less
In power and excellence, but favoured more   350
Of him who rules above; so was his will
Pronounced among the gods, and by an oath
That shook heaven's whole circumference, confirmed.
Thither let us bend all our thoughts, to learn
What creatures there inhabit, of what mould   355
Or substance, how endued, and what their power
And where their weakness; how attempted best
By force or subtlety; though heaven be shut,
And heaven's high arbitrator sit secure
In his own strength, this place may lie exposed,   360
The utmost border of his kingdom, left
To their defence who hold it: here perhaps
Some advantageous acts may be achieved
By sudden onset – either with hell-fire
To waste his whole creation, or possess   365
All as our own, and drive, as we are driven,
The puny habitants; or if not drive,
Seduce them to our party, that their God
May prove their foe, and with repenting hand
Abolish his own works. This would surpass   370
Common revenge, and interrupt his joy
In our confusion, and our joy upraise
In his disturbance; when his darling sons,
Hurled headlong to partake with us, shall curse
Their frail original, and faded bliss –   375
Faded so soon. Advise if this be worth
Attempting, or to sit in darkness here
Hatching vain empires.' Thus Beëlzebub
Pleaded his devilish counsel – first devised
By Satan, and in part proposed: for whence,   380
But from the author of all ill, could spring
So deep a malice, to confound the race
Of mankind in one root, and earth with hell
To mingle and involve, done all to spite
The great creator? But their spite still serves   385
His glory to augment. The bold design

Pleased highly those infernal states, and joy
Sparkled in all their eyes; with full assent
They vote: whereat his speech he thus renews:
'Well have ye judged, well ended long debate,   390
Synod of gods, and like to what ye are,
Great things resolved, which from the lowest deep
Will once more lift us up, in spite of fate,
Nearer our ancient seat – perhaps in view   394
Of those bright confines, whence, with neighbouring arms
And opportune excursion, we may chance
Re-enter heaven; or else in some mild zone
Dwell, not unvisited of heaven's fair light
Secure, and at the brightening orient beam
Purge off this gloom: the soft delicious air,   400
To heal the scar of these corrosive fires,
Shall breathe her balm. But, first, whom shall we send
In search of this new world, whom shall we find
Sufficient? Who shall tempt with wandering feet
The dark, unbottomed, infinite abyss,   405
And through the palpable obscure find out
His uncouth way, or spread his airy flight,
Upborne with indefatigable wings
Over the vast abrupt, ere he arrive
The happy isle? What strength, what art, can then   410
Suffice, or what evasion bear him safe,
Through the strict senteries and stations thick
Of angels watching round? Here he had need
All circumspection, and we now no less
Choice in our suffrage; for on whom we send   415
The weight of all, and our last hope, relies.'
    This said, he sat; and expectation held
His look suspense, awaiting who appeared
To second, or oppose, or undertake
The perilous attempt; but all sat mute,   420
Pondering the danger with deep thoughts; and each
In other's countenance read his own dismay,
Astonished; none among the choice and prime
Of those heaven-warring champions could be found
So hardy as to proffer or accept,   425
Alone, the dreadful voyage; till at last

Satan, whom now transcendent glory raised
Above his fellows, with monarchal pride
Conscious of highest worth, unmoved thus spake:
    'O progeny of heaven, empyreal thrones;   430
With reason hath deep silence and demur
Seized us, though undismayed; long is the way
And hard, that out of hell leads up to light;
Our prison strong, this huge convex of fire,
Outrageous to devour, immures us round   435
Ninefold; and gates of burning adamant,
Barred over us, prohibit all egress.
These passed, if any pass, the void profound
Of unessential night receives him next,
Wide gaping, and with utter loss of being   440
Threatens him, plunged in that abortive gulf.
If thence he scape, into whatever world,
Or unknown region, what remains him less
Than unknown dangers, and as hard escape?
But I should ill became this throne, O peers,   445
And this imperial sovereignty, adorned
With splendour, armed with power, if aught proposed
And judged of public moment in the shape
Of difficulty or danger, could deter
Me from attempting. Wherefore do I assume   450
These royalties, and not refuse to reign,
Refusing to accept as great a share
Of hazard as of honour, due alike
To him who reigns, and so much to him due
Of hazard more as he above the rest   455
High honoured sits? Go therefore mighty powers,
Terror of heaven, though fallen; intend at home,
While here shall be our home, what best may ease
The present misery, and render hell
More tolerable; if there be cure or charm   460
To respite or deceive, or slack the pain
Of this ill mansion: intermit no watch
Against a wakeful foe, while I abroad
Through all the coasts of dark destruction seek
Deliverance for us all; this enterprise   465
None shall partake with me.' Thus saying, rose

The monarch, and prevented all reply;
Prudent lest, from his resolution raised,
Others among the chief might offer now
(Certain to be refused) what erst they feared,   470
And so refused might in opinion stand
His rivals, winning cheap the high repute
Which he through hazard huge must earn. But they
Dreaded not more the adventure than his voice
Forbidding; and at once with him they rose;   475
Their rising all at once was as the sound
Of thunder heard remote. Towards him they bend
With awful reverence prone, and as a god
Extol him equal to the highest in heaven.
Nor failed they to express how much they praised   480
That for the general safety he despised
His own: for neither do the spirits damned
Lose all their virtue; lest bad men should boast
Their specious deeds on earth, which glory excites,
Or close ambition varnished o'er with zeal.   485
    Thus they their doubtful consultations dark
Ended, rejoicing in their matchless chief:
As, when from mountain tops the dusky clouds
Ascending, while the north wind sleeps, o'erspread
Heaven's cheerful face, the louring element   490
Scowls o'er the darkened landscape snow or shower,
If chance the radiant sun, with farewell sweet,
Extend his evening beam, the fields revive,
The birds their notes renew, and bleating herds
Attest their joy, that hill and valley rings.   495
O shame to men! Devil with devil damned
Firm concord holds; men only disagree
Of creatures rational, though under hope
Of heavenly grace, and, God proclaiming peace,
Yet live in hatred, enmity, and strife   500
Among themselves, and levy cruel wars
Wasting the earth, each other to destroy:
As if (which might induce us to accord)
Man had not hellish foes enow besides,
That day and night for his destruction wait.   505
    The Stygian council thus dissolved; and forth

In order came the grand infernal peers:
Midst came their mighty paramount, and seemed
Alone the antagonist of heaven, nor less
Than hell's dread emperor, with pomp supreme   510
And god-like imitated state; him round
A globe of fiery seraphim enclosed
With bright emblazonry, and horrent arms.
Then of their session ended they bid cry
With trumpets' regal sound the great result: 515
Toward the four winds four speedy cherubim
Put to their mouths the sounding alchemy,
By herald's voice explained; the hollow abyss
Heard far and wide, and all the host of hell
With deafening shout returned them loud acclaim.   520
Thence more at ease their minds, and somewhat raised
By false presumptuous hope, the rangèd powers
Disband; and, wandering, each his several way
Pursues, as inclination or sad choice
Leads him perplexed, where he may likeliest find   525
Truce to his restless thoughts, and entertain
The irksome hours, till his great chief return.
Part on the plain, or in the air sublime,
Upon the wing or in swift race contend,
As at the Olympian games or Pythian fields;   530
Part curb their fiery steeds, or shun the goal
With rapid wheels, or fronted brigades form:
As when, to warn proud cities, war appears
Waged in the troubled sky, and armies rush
To battle in the clouds; before each van   535
Prick forth the airy knights, and couch their spears,
Till thickest legions close; with feats of arms
From either end of heaven the welkin burns.
Others, with vast Typhoean rage, more fell,
Rend up both rocks and hills, and ride the air   540
In whirlwind; hell scarce holds the wild uproar:
As when Alcides, from Oechalia crowned
With conquest, felt the envenomed robe, and tore
Through pain up by the roots Thessalian pines,
And Lichas from the top of Oeta threw   545
Into the Euboic sea. Others, more mild,

Retreated in a silent valley, sing
With notes angelical to many a harp
Their own heroic deeds, and hapless fall
By doom of battle, and complain that fate   550
Free virtue should enthral to force or chance.
Their song was partial; but the harmony
(What could it less when spirits immortal sing?)
Suspended hell, and took with ravishment
The thronging audience. In discourse more sweet   555
(For eloquence the soul, song charms the sense)
Others apart sat on a hill retired,
In thoughts more elevate, and reasoned high
Of providence, foreknowledge, will, and fate –
Fixed fate, free will, foreknowledge absolute,   560
And found no end, in wandering mazes lost.
Of good and evil much they argued then,
Of happiness and final misery,
Passion and apathy, and glory and shame:
Vain wisdom all, and false philosophy –   565
Yet with a pleasing sorcery could charm
Pain for a while or anguish, and excite
Fallacious hope, or arm the obdurèd breast
With stubborn patience as with triple steel.
Another part, in squadrons and gross bands,   570
On bold adventure to discover wide
That dismal world, if any clime perhaps
Might yield them easier habitation, bend
Four ways their flying march, along the banks
Of four infernal rivers, that disgorge   575
Into the burning lake their baleful streams –
Abhorrèd Styx, the flood of deadly hate;
Sad Acheron of sorrow, black and deep;
Cocytus, named of lamentation loud
Heard on the rueful stream; fierce Phlegethon,   580
Whose waves of torrent fire inflame with rage.
Far off from these, a slow and silent stream,
Lethe, the river of oblivion, rolls
Her watery labyrinth, whereof who drinks
Forthwith his former state and being forgets –   585
Forgets both joy and grief, pleasure and pain.

Beyond this flood a frozen continent
Lies dark and wild, beat with perpetual storms
Of whirlwind and dire hail, which on firm land
Thaws not, but gathers heap, and ruin seems   590
Of ancient pile; all else deep snow and ice,
A gulf profound as that Serbonian bog
Betwixt Damiata and Mount Casius old,
Where armies whole have sunk: the parching air
Burns frore, and cold performs the effect of fire.   595
Thither, by harpy-footed Furies haled,
At certain revolutions all the damned
Are brought; and feel by turns the bitter change
Of fierce extremes, extremes by change more fierce,
From beds of raging fire to starve in ice   600
Their soft ethereal warmth, and there to pine
Immovable, infixed, and frozen round
Periods of time – thence hurried back to fire.
They ferry over this Lethean sound
Both to and fro, their sorrow to augment,   605
And wish and struggle, as they pass, to reach
The tempting stream, with one small drop to lose
In sweet forgetfulness all pain and woe,
All in one moment, and so near the brink;
But fate withstands, and, to oppose the attempt,   610
Medusa with Gorgonian terror guards
The ford, and of itself the water flies
All taste of living wight, as once it fled
The lip of Tantalus. Thus roving on
In confused march forlorn, the adventurous bands   615
With shuddering horror pale, and eyes aghast,
Viewed first their lamentable lot, and found
No rest; through many a dark and dreary vale
They passed, and many a region dolorous,
O'er many a frozen, many a fiery alp,   620
Rocks, caves, lakes, fens, bogs, dens, and shades of death –
A universe of death, which God by curse
Created evil, for evil only good;
Where all life dies, death lives, and nature breeds,
Perverse, all monstrous, all prodigious things,   625
Abominable, inutterable, and worse

Than fables yet have feigned or fear conceived,
Gorgons, and Hydras, and Chimeras dire.
  Meanwhile the adversary of God and man,
Satan, with thoughts inflamed of highest design,   630
Puts on swift wings, and toward the gates of hell
Explores his solitary flight; sometimes
He scours the right hand coast, sometimes the left;
Now shaves with level wing the deep, then soars
Up to the fiery concave towering high.   635
As when far off at sea a fleet descried
Hangs in the clouds, by equinoctial winds
Close sailing from Bengala, or the isles
Of Ternate and Tidore, whence merchants bring
Their spicy drugs; they on the trading flood,   640
Through the wide Ethiopian to the Cape,
Ply stemming nightly toward the pole: so seemed
Far off the flying fiend; at last appear
Hell-bounds, high reaching to the horrid roof,
And thrice threefold the gates; three folds were brass,   645
Three iron, three of adamantine rock,
Impenetrable, impaled with circling fire,
Yet unconsumed. Before the gates there sat
On either side a formidable shape;
The one seemed woman to the waist, and fair,   650
But ended foul in many a scaly fold,
Voluminous and vast – a serpent armed
With mortal sting; about her middle round
A cry of hell hounds never ceasing barked
With wide Cerberean mouths full loud, and rung   655
A hideous peal; yet, when they list, would creep,
If aught disturbed their noise, into her womb,
And kennel there; yet there still barked and howled
Within unseen. Far less abhorred than these
Vexed Scylla, bathing in the sea that parts   660
Calabria from the hoarse Trinacrian shore;
Nor uglier follow the night-hag, when, called
In secret, riding through the air she comes,
Lured with the smell of infant blood, to dance
With Lapland witches, while the labouring moon   665
Eclipses at their charms. The other shape –

If shape it might be called that shape had none
Distinguishable in member, joint, or limb;
Or substance might be called that shadow seemed,
For each seemed either – black it stood as night,   670
Fierce as ten Furies, terrible as hell,
And shook a dreadful dart: what seemed his head
The likeness of a kingly crown had on.
Satan was now at hand, and from his seat
The monster moving onward came as fast   675
With horrid strides; hell trembled as he strode.
The undaunted fiend what this might be admired,
Admired, not feared – God and his Son except,
Created thing nought valued he nor shunned –
And with disdainful look thus first began: 680
    'Whence and what art thou, execrable shape,
That dar'st, though grim and terrible, advance
Thy miscreated front athwart my way
To yonder gates? Through them I mean to pass,
That be assured, without leave asked of thee: 685
Retire, or taste thy folly, and learn by proof,
Hell-born, not to contend with spirits of heaven.'
    To whom the goblin, full of wrath, replied:
'Art thou that traitor angel, art thou he,
Who first broke peace in heaven and faith, till then   690
Unbroken, and in proud rebellious arms
Drew after him the third part of heaven's sons,
Conjured against the highest – for which both thou
And they outcast from God, are here condemned
To waste eternal days in woe and pain?   695
And reckon'st thou thyself with spirits of heaven,
Hell-doomed, and breath'st defiance here and scorn,
Where I reign king, and to enrage thee more,
Thy king and lord? Back to thy punishment,
False fugitive, and to thy speed add wings,   700
Lest with a whip of scorpions I pursue
Thy lingering, or with one stroke of this dart
Strange horror seize thee, and pangs unfelt before.'
    So spake the grisly terror, and in shape,
So speaking and so threatening, grew tenfold   705
More dreadful and deform; on the other side,

Incensed with indignation, Satan stood
Unterrified, and like a comet burned,
That fires the length of Ophiucus huge
In the arctic sky, and from his horrid hair   710
Shakes pestilence and war. Each at the head
Levelled his deadly aim; their fatal hands
No second stroke intend; and such a frown
Each cast at the other as when two black clouds,
With heaven's artillery fraught, come rattling on   715
Over the Caspian – then stand front to front
Hovering a space, till winds the signal blow
To join their dark encounter in mid air;
So frowned the mighty combatants that hell
Grew darker at their frown; so matched they stood;   720
For never but once more was either like
To meet so great a foe; and now great deeds
Had been achieved, whereof all hell had rung,
Had not the snaky sorceress, that sat
Fast by hell gate and kept the fatal key,   725
Risen, and with hideous outcry rushed between.
   'O father, what intends thy hand,' she cried,
'Against thy only son? What fury, O son,
Possesses thee to bend that mortal dart
Against thy father's head? And know'st for whom?   730
For him who sits above, and laughs the while
At thee, ordained his drudge to execute
Whate'er his wrath, which he calls justice, bids –
His wrath, which one day will destroy ye both.'
   She spake, and at her words the hellish pest   735
Forbore; then these to her Satan returned:
   'So strange thy outcry, and thy words so strange
Thou interposest, that my sudden hand,
Prevented, spares to tell thee yet by deeds
What it intends, till first I know of thee   740
What thing thou art, thus double-formed, and why,
In this infernal vale first met, thou call'st
Me father, and that phantasm call'st my son.
I know thee not, nor ever saw till now
Sight more detestable than him and thee.'   745
   To whom thus the portress of hell gate replied:

'Hast thou forgot me, then; and do I seem
Now in thine eye so foul? – once deemed so fair
In heaven, when at the assembly, and in sight
Of all the seraphim with thee combined   750
In bold conspiracy against heaven's king,
All on a sudden miserable pain
Surprised thee, dim thine eyes and dizzy swum
In darkness, while thy head flames thick and fast
Threw forth, till on the left side opening wide,   755
Likest to thee in shape and countenance bright,
Then shining heavenly fair, a goddess armed,
Out of thy head I sprung; amazement seized
All the host of heaven: back they recoiled afraid
At first, and called me Sin, and for a sign   760
Portentous held me; but, familiar grown,
I pleased, and with attractive graces won
The most averse – thee chiefly, who, full oft
Thyself in me thy perfect image viewing,
Becam'st enamoured; and such joy thou took'st   765
With me in secret that my womb conceived
A growing burden. Meanwhile war arose,
And fields were fought in heaven: wherein remained
(For what could else?) to our almighty foe
Clear victory; to our part loss and rout   770
Through all the empyrean; down they fell,
Driven headlong from the pitch of heaven, down
Into this deep, and in the general fall
I also: at which time this powerful key
Into my hand was given, with charge to keep   775
These gates for ever shut, which none can pass
Without my opening. Pensive here I sat
Alone; but long I sat not, till my womb,
Pregnant by thee, and now excessive grown,
Prodigious motion felt and rueful throes.   780
At last this odious offspring whom thou seest,
Thine own begotten, breaking violent way,
Tore through my entrails, that with fear and pain
Distorted, all my nether shape thus grew
Transformed: but he my inbred enemy   785
Forth issued, brandishing his fatal dart,

Made to destroy: I fled, and cried out "Death";
Hell trembled at the hideous name, and sighed
From all her caves, and back resounded "Death".
I fled, but he pursued (though more, it seems,   790
Inflamed with lust than rage) and swifter far,
Me overtook, his mother, all dismayed,
And, in embraces forcible and foul
Engendering with me, of that rape begot
These yelling monsters, that with ceaseless cry   795
Surround me, as thou saw'st – hourly conceived
And hourly born, with sorrow infinite
To me; for, when they list, into the womb
That bred them they return, and howl, and gnaw
My bowels, their repast; then, bursting forth   800
Afresh, with conscious terrors vex me round,
That rest or intermission none I find.
Before mine eyes in opposition sits
Grim Death, my son and foe, who sets them on,
And me, his parent, would full soon devour   805
For want of other prey, but that he knows
His end with mine involved, and knows that I
Should prove a bitter morsel, and his bane,
Whenever that shall be: so Fate pronounced.
But thou, O father, I forewarn thee, shun   810
His deadly arrow; neither vainly hope
To be invulnerable in those bright arms,
Though tempered heavenly; for that mortal dint,
Save he who reigns above, none can resist.'
    She finished, and the subtle fiend his lore   815
Soon learned, now milder, and thus answered smooth:
'Dear daughter – since thou claim'st me for thy sire,
And my fair son here show'st me, the dear pledge
Of dalliance had with thee in heaven, and joys
Then sweet, now sad to mention, through dire change   820
Befallen us unforeseen, unthought-of – know
I come no enemy, but to set free
From out this dark and dismal house of pain
Both him and thee, and all the heavenly host
Of spirits that, in our just pretences armed,   825
Fell with us from on high; from them I go

This uncouth errand sole, and one for all
Myself expose, with lonely steps to tread
The unfounded deep, and through the void immense
To search, with wandering quest, a place foretold   830
Should be – and, by concurring signs, ere now
Created vast and round – a place of bliss
In the purlieus of heaven; and therein placed
A race of upstart creatures, to supply
Perhaps our vacant room, though more removed,   835
Lest heaven, surcharged with potent multitude,
Might hap to move new broils; be this, or aught
Than this more secret, now designed, I haste
To know; and this once known, shall soon return,
And bring ye to the place where thou and Death   840
Shall dwell at ease, and up and down unseen
Wing silently the buxom air, embalmed
With odours; there ye shall be fed and filled
Immeasurably: all things shall be your prey.'
     He ceased, for both seemed highly pleased, and Death 845
Grinned horrible a ghastly smile, to hear
His famine should be filled, and blessed his maw
Destined to that good hour; no less rejoiced
His mother bad, and thus bespake her sire:
     'The key of this infernal pit, by due   850
And by command of heaven's all-powerful king,
I keep, by him forbidden to unlock
These adamantine gates; against all force
Death ready stands to interpose his dart,
Fearless to be o'ermatched by living might.   855
But what owe I to his commands above,
Who hates me, and hath hither thrust me down
Into this gloom of Tartarus profound,
To sit in hateful office here confined,
Inhabitant of heaven and heavenly born –   860
Here in perpetual agony and pain,
With terrors and with clamours compassed round
Of mine own brood, that on my bowels feed?
Thou art my father, thou my author, thou
My being gav'st me; whom should I obey   865
But thee, whom follow? Thou wilt bring me soon

To that new world of light and bliss, among
The gods who live at ease, where I shall reign
At thy right hand voluptuous, as beseems
Thy daughter and thy darling, without end.' 870
    Thus saying, from her side the fatal key,
Sad instrument of all our woe, she took;
And, towards the gate rolling her bestial train,
Forthwith the huge portcullis high updrew,
Which, but herself, not all the Stygian powers 875
Could once have moved; then in the key-hole turns
The intricate wards, and every bolt and bar
Of massy iron or solid rock with ease
Unfastens; on a sudden open fly,
With impetuous recoil and jarring sound, 880
The infernal doors, and on their hinges grate
Harsh thunder, that the lowest bottom shook
Of Erebus. She opened, but to shut
Excelled her power: the gates wide open stood,
That with extended wings a bannered host, 885
Under spread ensigns marching, might pass through
With horse and chariots ranked in loose array;
So wide they stood, and like a furnace-mouth
Cast forth redounding smoke and ruddy flame.
Before their eyes in sudden view appear 890
The secrets of the hoary deep – a dark
Illimitable ocean without bound,
Without dimension; where length, breadth, and height,
And time and place, are lost; where eldest Night
And Chaos, ancestors of Nature, hold 895
Eternal anarchy, amidst the noise
Of endless wars, and by confusion stand.
For Hot, Cold, Moist, and Dry, four champions fierce,
Strive here for mastery, and to battle bring
Their embryon atoms: they around the flag 900
Of each his faction, in their several clans,
Light-armed or heavy, sharp, smooth, swift, or slow,
Swarm populous, unnumbered as the sands
Of Barca or Cyrene's torrid soil,
Levied to side with warring winds, and poise 905
Their lighter wings. To whom these most adhere

He rules a moment: Chaos umpire sits,
And by decision more embroils the fray
By which he reigns; next him, high arbiter,
Chance governs all. Into this wild abyss,   910
The womb of Nature, and perhaps her grave,
Of neither sea, nor shore, nor air, nor fire,
But all these in their pregnant causes mixed
Confusedly, and which thus must ever fight,
Unless the almighty maker them ordain   915
His dark materials to create more worlds –
Into this wild abyss the wary fiend
Stood on the brink of hell and looked a while,
Pondering his voyage; for no narrow frith
He had to cross. Nor was his ear less pealed   920
With noises loud and ruinous (to compare
Great things with small) than when Bellona storms
With all her battering engines, bent to raze
Some capital city; or less than if this frame
Of heaven were falling, and these elements   925
In mutiny had from her axle torn
The steadfast earth. At last his sail-broad vans
He spreads for flight, and, in the surging smoke
Uplifted, spurns the ground; thence many a league,
As in a cloudy chair, ascending rides   930
Audacious, but that seat soon failing, meets
A vast vacuity; all unawares,
Fluttering his pennons vain, plumb-down he drops
Ten thousand fathom deep, and to this hour
Down had been falling, had not by ill chance   935
The strong rebuff of some tumultuous cloud,
Instinct with fire and nitre, hurried him
As many miles aloft; that fury stayed –
Quenched in a boggy Syrtis, neither sea,
Nor good dry land – nigh foundered, on he fares,   940
Treading the crude consistence, half on foot,
Half flying; behoves him now both oar and sail.
As when a griffin through the wilderness
With wingèd course, o'er hill or moory dale,
Pursues the Arimaspian, who by stealth   945
Had from his wakeful custody purloined

The guarded gold; so eagerly the fiend
O'er bog or steep, through strait, rough, dense, or rare,
With head, hands, wings or feet, pursues his way,
And swims, or sinks, or wades, or creeps, or flies;   950
At length a universal hubbub wild
Of stunning sounds, and voices all confused,
Borne through the hollow dark, assaults his ear
With loudest vehemence; thither he plies
Undaunted, to meet there whatever power   955
Or spirit of the nethermost abyss
Might in that noise reside, of whom to ask
Which way the nearest coast of darkness lies
Bordering on light; when straight behold the throne
Of Chaos, and his dark pavilion spread   960
Wide on the wasteful deep; with him enthroned
Sat sable-vested Night, eldest of things,
The consort of his reign; and by them stood
Orcus and Ades, and the dreaded name
Of Demogorgon; Rumour next, and Chance,   965
And Tumult and Confusion, all embroiled,
And Discord with a thousand various mouths.
     To whom Satan, turning boldly, thus: 'Ye powers
And spirits of this nethermost abyss,
Chaos and ancient Night, I come no spy   970
With purpose to explore or to disturb
The secrets of your realm, but by constraint
Wandering this darksome desert, as my way
Lies through your spacious empire up to light
Alone and without guide, half lost, I seek   975
What readiest path leads where your gloomy bounds
Confine with heaven; or if some other place,
From your dominion won, the ethereal king
Possesses lately, thither to arrive
I travel this profound; direct my course: 980
Directed, no mean recompense it brings
To your behoof, if I that region lost,
All usurpation thence expelled, reduce
To her original darkness and your sway
(Which is my present journey) and once more   985
Erect the standard there of ancient Night.

Yours be the advantage all, mine the revenge.'
    Thus Satan; and him thus the anarch old,
With faltering speech and visage incomposed,
Answered: 'I know thee, stranger, who thou art –   990
That mighty leading angel, who of late
Made head against heaven's king, though overthrown.
I saw and heard; for such a numerous host
Fled not in silence through the frighted deep,
With ruin upon ruin, rout on rout,   995
Confusion worse confounded; and heaven gates
Poured out by millions her victorious bands,
Pursuing. I upon my frontiers here
Keep residence; if all I can will serve
That little which is left so to defend,   1000
Encroached on still through our intestine broils
Weakening the sceptre of old Night: first hell,
Your dungeon, stretching far and wide beneath;
Now lately heaven and earth, another world
Hung o'er my realm, linked in a golden chain   1005
To that side heaven from whence your legions fell;
If that way be your walk, you have not far;
So much the nearer danger; go, and speed;
Havoc and spoil and ruin are my gain.'
    He ceased; and Satan stayed not to reply,   1010
But glad that now his sea should find a shore,
With fresh alacrity and force renewed
Springs upward, like a pyramid of fire,
Into the wild expanse, and through the shock
Of fighting elements, on all sides round   1015
Environed, wins his way; harder beset
And more endangered than when Argo passed
Through Bosporus betwixt the jostling rocks,
Or when Ulysses on the larboard shunned
Charybdis, and by the other whirlpool steered.   1020
So he with difficulty and labour hard
Moved on, with difficulty and labour he;
But, he once passed, soon after, when man fell,
Strange alteration! Sin and Death amain,
Following his track – such was the will of heaven –   1025
Paved after him a broad and beaten way

Over the dark abyss, whose boiling gulf
Tamely endured a bridge of wondrous length,
From hell continued, reaching the utmost orb
Of this frail world; by which the spirits perverse   1030
With easy intercourse pass to and fro
To tempt or punish mortals, except whom
God and good angels guard by special grace.
    But now at last the sacred influence
Of light appears, and from the walls of heaven   1035
Shoots far into the bosom of dim Night
A glimmering dawn; here Nature first begins
Her farthest verge, and Chaos to retire,
As from her outmost works, a broken foe,
With tumult less and with less hostile din;   1040
That Satan with less toil, and now with ease,
Wafts on the calmer wave by dubious light,
And, like a weather-beaten vessel, holds
Gladly the port, though shrouds and tackle torn;
Or in the emptier waste, resembling air,   1045
Weighs his spread wings, at leisure to behold
Far off the empyreal heaven, extended wide
In circuit, undetermined square or round,
With opal towers and battlements adorned
Of living sapphire, once his native seat;   1050
And, fast by, hanging in a golden chain,
This pendent world, in bigness as a star
Of smallest magnitude close by the moon.
Thither, full fraught with mischievous revenge,
Accursed, and in a cursed hour, he hies.   1055

THE END OF THE SECOND BOOK

Samson Agonistes

Samson's speech
before the prison in Gaza

A little onward lend thy guiding hand
To these dark steps, a little further on;
For yonder bank hath choice of sun or shade;
There I am wont to sit, when any chance
Relieves me from my task of servile toil,   5
Daily in the common prison else enjoined me,
Where I, a prisoner chained, scarce freely draw
The air, imprisoned also, close and damp,
Unwholesome draught; but here I feel amends –
The breath of heaven fresh blowing, pure and sweet,   10
With day-spring born; here leave me to respire.
This day a solemn feast the people hold
To Dagon, their sea-idol, and forbid
Laborious works; unwillingly this rest
Their superstition yields me; hence, with leave   15
Retiring from the popular noise, I seek
This unfrequented place, to find some ease –
Ease to the body some, none to the mind
From restless thoughts, that like a deadly swarm
Of hornets armed, no sooner found alone   20
But rush upon me thronging, and present
Times past, what once I was, and what am now.
Oh, wherefore was my birth from heaven foretold
Twice by an angel, who at last, in sight
Of both my parents, all in flames ascended   25
From off the altar where an offering burned,
As in a fiery column charioting
His godlike presence, and from some great act
Or benefit revealed to Abraham's race?
Why was my breeding ordered and prescribed   30
As of a person separate to God,

Designed for great exploits, if I must die
Betrayed, captived, and both my eyes put out,
Made of my enemies the scorn and gaze,
To grind in brazen fetters under task   35
With this heaven-gifted strength? O glorious strength,
Put to the labour of a beast, debased
Lower than bond-slave! Promise was that I
Should Israel from Philistian yoke deliver;
Ask for this great deliverer now, and find him   40
Eyeless in Gaza, at the mill with slaves,
Himself in bonds under Philistian yoke;
Yet stay; let me not rashly call in doubt
Divine prediction; what if all foretold
Had been fulfilled but through mine own default?   45
Whom have I to complain of but myself?
Who this high gift of strength committed to me,
In what part lodged, how easily bereft me,
Under the seal of silence could not keep,
But weakly to a woman must reveal it,   50
O'ercome with importunity and tears?
O impotence of mind in body strong!
But what is strength without a double share
Of wisdom? Vast, unwieldy, burdensome,
Proudly secure, yet liable to fall   55
By weakest subtleties; not made to rule,
But to subserve where wisdom bears command.
God, when he gave me strength, to show withal,
How slight the gift was, hung it in my hair.
But peace, I must not quarrel with the will   60
Of highest dispensation, which herein
Haply had ends above my reach to know;
Suffices that to me strength is my bane,
And proves the source of all my miseries –
So many, and so huge, that each apart   65
Would ask a life to wail; but, chief of all,
O loss of sight, of thee I most complain!
Blind among enemies, O worse than chains,
Dungeon, or beggary, or decrepit age!
Light, the prime work of God, to me is extinct,   70
And all her various objects of delight

Annulled, which might in part my grief have eased;
Inferior to the vilest now become
Of man or worm, the vilest here excel me:
They creep, yet see; I, dark in light, exposed   75
To daily fraud, contempt, abuse, and wrong,
Within doors, or without, still as a fool,
In power of others, never in my own –
Scarce half I seem to live, dead more than half.
O dark, dark, dark, amid the blaze of noon,   80
Irrecoverably dark, total eclipse
Without all hope of day!
O first-created beam, and thou great word,
'Let there be light, and light was over all,'
Why am I thus bereaved thy prime decree?   85
The sun to me is dark
And silent as the moon,
When she deserts the night,
Hid in her vacant interlunar cave.
Since light so necessary is to life,   90
And almost life itself, if it be true
That light is in the soul,
She all in every part, why was the sight
To such a tender ball as the eye confined,
So obvious and so easy to be quenched,   95
And not, as feeling, through all parts diffused,
That she might look at will through every pore?
Then had I not been thus exiled from light,
As in the land of darkness, yet in light,
To live a life half dead, a living death,   100
And buried; but O yet more miserable!
Myself my sepulchre, a moving grave;
Buried, yet not exempt,
By privilege of death and burial,
From worst of other evils, pains, and wrongs;   105
But made hereby obnoxious more
To all the miseries of life,
Life in captivity
Among inhuman foes.

Notes

On Time **1.3 plummet:** the weight (not the pendulum) of a clock. **l.4: womb:** stomach. **l.9 when as:** when. **l.12 individual:** insepara-ble.**l.14 sincerely:** wholly.

At a Solemn Music **1.6 concent:** harmony. **l.23 diapason:** harmony.

L'Allegro 'L'Allegro' and 'Il Penseroso' cannot be dated precisely, but they may have been written while Milton was in Hammersmith (1632–5) or Horton (1635–8). **L'Allegro:** the phrase is Italian, and means 'the cheerful man'. **1.5 uncouth cell:** desolate cave. **l.8 shades:** trees. **l.12 yclept:** called. **l.24 buxom:** yielding. **l.27 cranks:** jokes dependent on verbal twists. **l.28 becks:** upward nods corresponding to a beckoning by hand. **l.33 trip:** move lightly. **l.60 state:** stately progress. **l.62 dight:** clothed. **l.67 tells his tale:** either 'counts his sheep' or 'tells his story'. **l.91 secure:** carefree. **l.94 rebecks:** early bowed instruments. **l.104 friar's lantern:** the will-o'-the-wisp. **l.110 lubber:** drudging. **l.111 chimney:** fireplace. **l.120 weeds:** clothes. **l.120 triumphs:** pageants or spectacles. **11.121–2:** the bright eyes are compared to stars, the ethereal fluid of which rains on mankind, thus controlling character and destiny. **l.132 sock:** low-heeled slipper worn by Greek comic actors.

Il Penseroso **Il Penseroso:** the phrase is Italian, and means 'the contemplative man'. **l.3 bestead:** help. **l.10 pensioners:** attendants. **l.33 grain:** colour. **l.35 cypress lawn:** fine black linen. **l.43 sad:** serious. **l.55 hist:** to call with the exclamation 'hist'. **1.73 plat:** plot. **l.77 air:** weather. **l.83 bellman's drowsy charm:** night-watchman's drowsy chant. **l.87 outwatch the Bear:** stay up all night. The Bear (Ursa Major) never sets. **l.102 buskined:** the buskin was a high boot worn by Greek tragic actors. **l.127 still:** quiet. **l.130 minute:** falling at intervals of one minute. **l.145 consort:** musical harmony. **l.156 pale:** enclosure. **l.157 embowèd:** vaulted. **l.158 antique:** may mean 'old' or 'fantastic, grotesque'. **l.158 massy-proof:** massive, and proof against the weight of the roof. **l.159 storied:** depicting Biblical stories. **ll.170–1 spell/Of:** interpret.

Comus **l.4   serene:** clear, bright. **l.7 pestered:** crowded. **l.7 pinfold:** animal pound. **l.16 ambrosial weeds:** immortal clothes. **l.24 grace:** honour. **l.37 perplexed:** entangled. **l.65 orient:** bright. **l.66 drought of Phoebus:** thirst caused by the sun. **l.83 Iris' woof:** the woven fabric of the rainbow, of which Iris was the goddess. **l.92 viewless:** invisible. **l.93 star:** Hesperus, the evening star. **l.95 car of day:** the chariot of the sun. **l.97 stream:** the ancients believed that the earth was encircled by a river, Oceanus. **l.110 saws:** sententious sayings. **l.117 shelves:** sandbanks or shallows. **l.151 trains:** deceits. **l.154 spongy:** absorbent. **l.161 glozing:** flattering. **l.165 virtue:** power, efficacy. **l.168 fairly:** quietly. **l.174 loose unlettered hinds:** dissolute and illiterate rustics. **l.197 dark lantern:** a lantern, the light from which can be darkened with a shutter. **l.212 siding:** supporting. **l.241 parley:** speech. **l.251 fall:** cadence. **l.262 home-felt:** intimately felt. **l.267 Unless the goddess:** unless you are the goddess. **l.293 swinked:** tired. **l.297 port:** deportment, bearing. **l.301 plighted:** plaited, interwoven. **l.312 Dingle:** wooden hollow. **l.313 bosky bourn:** small stream overhung with bushes. **l.315 attendance:** attendants. **l.318 thatched pallet:** straw bed. **l.332 benison:** blessing. **l.359 over-exquisite:** too precise. **l.360 cast:** forecast. **l.366 to seek:** deficient. **l.380 to:** an archaic intensive prefix. **l.382 centre:** of the earth. **l.386 affects:** loves. **l.404 it recks me not:** I am not concerned. **l.407 unownèd:** lost. **l.411 arbitrate the event:** decide the outcome. **l.423 unharboured:** offering no shelter. **l.433 fire:** will-o'-the-wisp. **l.444 pard:** leopard. **l.465 lavish:** licentious. **l.468 Embodies, and imbrutes:** becomes corporeal and bestial. **l.479 crude:** indigestible. **l.483 night-foundered:** engulfed in night. **l.491 stakes:** swords. **l.509 sadly:** seriously. **l.533 monstrous rout:** rout of monsters. **l.542 dew-besprent:** sprinkled with dew. **l.585 period:** sentence. **l.586 for me:** for my part. **l.598 pillared firmament:** the dome of the sky supported by pillars. **l.620 to see to:** to look at. **l.621 virtuous:** efficacious. **l.626 scrip:** bag. **l.627 simples:** medicinal herbs. **l.628 faculties:** properties. **l.635 clouted shoon:** shoes protected with iron plates, or studded with large-headed nails. **l.636 moly:** plant given to Ulysses to protect him from Circe. **l.646 lime-twigs:** twigs smeared with bird-lime for trapping birds. **l.672 julep:** a sweet drink. **l.700 liquorish:** pleasant to the palate. **l.722 frieze:** coarse woollen cloth. **l.733 deep:** centre of the earth, the 'forehead' of which is the roof of the inside of the earth. **l.734 they below:** the spirits of the underworld. **l.750 grain:** hue. **l.757 juggler:** sorcerer. **l.759 pranked:** showily dressed. **l.760 bolt:** may mean 'refine', or 'utter hastily'. **l.791 fence:** the art of fencing. **l.793 uncontrollèd:** indisputable. **l.797 nerves:** sinews. **l.809 lees:** sediment. **l.823 soothest:** most truthful. **l.836 lank:** drooping. **l.838 lavers:** basins. **l.838 asphodel:** the immortal flower of the Elysian fields. **l.845 urchin blasts:** infections breathed by mischievous fairies. **l.970 timely:** early. **l.972 assays:** tests and tribulations. **l.980 liquid:** clear, bright. **l.984 crispèd:** ruffled. **l.990 cedarn:** composed of cedars. **l.995 purfled:** variegated. **l.1004 advanced:** elevated. **l.1015 bowed welkin:** the curved vault of the sky.

Lycidas On 10 August 1637 Edward King, a Fellow of Christ's College, Cambridge, was drowned. Milton dated his pastoral elegy 'November, 1637' in the Trinity MS, and published it the following year in a commemorative volume entitled *Justa Eduardo King*, a collection of poems in Latin, Greek and English written by King's Cambridge contemporaries. **l.2 sere:** dry, withered. **l.3 crude:** unripe. **l.4 rude:** unskilled. **l.13 welter:** writhe. **l.14 meed:** reward. **l.22 sable:** black. **l.48 blows:** blooms. **l.64 boots:** avails, profits. **l.79 foil:** the setting of a jewel. **l.91 felon:** savage, wild. **l.106 flower:** the hyacinth. **l.107 pledge:** child. **l.109 pilot:** St Peter, who was a Galilean fisherman when Jesus called him. **l.111 amain:** with full force. **l.112 mitred:** St Peter was the first bishop of the church, and so wears a mitre. **l.114 Enow:** plural of 'enough'. **l.122 sped:** satisfied. **l.123 list:** choose, desire. **l.123 flashy:** trifling, destitute of solidity or purpose. **l.124 scrannel:** thin, weak. **l.136 use:** go habitually. **l.138 swart star:** Sirius, the Dog Star, the heliacal rising of which occurs in midsummer. 'Swart' (blackened by heat) has been transferred from effect to cause. **l.142 rathe:** early. **l.158 monstrous world:** the world of sea-monsters. **l.161:** according to a Cornish legend, in the year 495 St Michael appeared to some fishermen who saw him standing on the Mount that now bears his name. **l.163 ruth:** pity. **l.168 day-star:** the sun. **l.170 tricks:** adorns. **l.173 him:** Jesus. See Matthew xiv. 25–31. **l.176 unexpressive:** inexpressible. **l.189 Doric lay:** pastoral song.

Sonnets **Sonnet I l.9 bird of hate:** the cuckoo. **Sonnet VII l.10 still:** forever. **Sonnet VIII:** After the Battle of Edgehill on 23 October 1642 the Parliamentary army retreated to Warwick, thus leaving the road to London open to the army of Charles, who advanced as far as Turnham Green, which was only a few miles from Milton's house on Aldersgate Street. The prospect of the fall of London may have occasioned the poem. **l.10 Emathian**

conqueror: Alexander the Great. **Sonnet XVIII:** The sect known as the Vaudois or Waldenses were believed by seventeenth-century Protestants to represent the continuity of Protestantism from earliest times to the Reformation. On 24 April 1655 the army of the Duke of Savoy, which consisted of French and Irish troops, began the mutilation, torture and slaughter of the members of the sect, and a few days later over 1,700 Vaudois were dead. Protestant Europe was outraged and Cromwell protested to the Duke of Savoy with a letter written by Milton.

Paradise Lost

Book I **l.1 fruit:** means 'fruit' and 'result'. **l.4 greater man:** Jesus. **l.8 shepherd:** Moses. **l.57 witnessed:** bore witness to. **l.72 utter:** outer. **l.114 Doubted:** feared for. **l.128 powers:** one of the orders of angels; seraphim (1.129) and cherubin (1.157) are other orders. **l.167 fail:** err. **l.187 offend:** injure. **l.208 Invests:** covers, envelops. **l.224 horrid:** the primary sense is 'bristling' (with 'pointing spires'), but the word probably carries the secondary sense of 'abominable'. **l.235 Sublimed:** an alchemical term meaning 'vaporised'. **l.285 Ethereal temper:** tempered by celestial fire. **ll.288–91:** the 'Tuscan artist' (i.e. scientist) is Galileo, whom Milton visited in 1638 or 1639. **l.294 ammiral:** flagship. **l.296 marl:** a kind of soil. **l.299 Nathless:** nevertheless. **l.339 Amran's son:** Moses. **l.372 religions:** religious rites. **l.411 Asphaltic Pool:** Dead Sea. **l.444 king:** Solomon, whose wives 'turned away his heart after other gods' (I Kings xi. 1–8). **l.460 groundsel:** threshold. **l.471 king:** Ahaz; see II Kings xvi. **l.484 rebel king:** Jeroboam. **l.502 flown:** archaic past-participle of 'flow' (not 'fly'). **l.508 Javan:** the grandson of Noah (Gen. x. 1–5). **l.543 reign:** realm. **l.550 Dorian mood:** one of the musical modes of ancient Greece, characterized by simplicity and solemnity. **l.551 flutes:** the Spartan army went into battle to the music of the flute (whereas the Romans used trumpets). **l.555 swage:** assuage. **l.575 small infantry:** pygmies. **l.580 Uther's son:** King Arthur. **l.597 disastrous:** foreboding disaster. **l.603 considerate:** considered, deliberate. **l.609 amerced:** deprived. **l.636 different:** may mean 'differing' or 'procrastinating'. **l.679 erected:** exalted. **l.694** alludes to the tower of Babel and the pyramids of Egypt. **l.765 paynim:** pagan. **l.766 career:** a charge or encounter at a tournament. **l.769 the sun with Taurus rides:** the sun enters the zodiacal sign of Taurus in April. **l.774 expatiate:** to walk about at large.

l.795 close recess: secret meeting-place. **l.795 conclave:** here used to refer to an assembly of cardinals who have met to elect a pope. **l.797 Frequent:** crowded.

Book II **1.9 success:** result. **l.106 denounced:** portended. **l.124 fact:** feat of valour or skill. **l.156 Belike:** in all likelihood. **l.165 What:** what about the occasion. **l.165 amain:** in haste. **l.218 temper:** temperament. **l.220 light:** means both 'brighter' and 'easier to bear'. **l.224 For happy:** in terms of happiness. **l.238 publish:** announce. **ll.249–51:** the object of 'pursue' is 'state'. **l.278 sensible:** perception through the senses. **l.297 policy:** statesmanship. **l.302 front:** forehead or face. **l.312 style:** ceremonial designation. **l.336 to:** to the limit of. **l.367 puny:** means 'born later' (*puis né*), 'inferior in rank' and 'weak'. **l.375 original:** progenitor, i.e. Adam. **l.376 Advise:** ponder. **l.387 states:** the 'estates' of Parliament. **l.391 Synod:** means 'assembly of clergy' and secondarily, 'conjunction of stars'. **l.404 tempt:** risk the perils of. **l.407 uncouth:** unknown. **l.409 abrupt:** abyss. **l.412 senteries:** sentries. **l.434 convex:** the vault of hell. **l.439 unessential:** without being, uncreated (cf. 1.150). **l.441 abortive:** rendering fruitless. **l.452 Refusing:** if I refuse. **l.457 intend:** consider. **l.461 deceive:** beguile. **l. 468 raised:** inspired with courage. **l.478 awful:** full of awe. **l.504 enow:** enough. **l.512 globe:** used in the Latin sense of 'a throng of people'. **l.513 emblazonry:** heraldic devices. **l.517 alchemy:** brass (i.e. trumpets). **l.522 powers:** here means 'armies'. **l.552 partial:** biased. **l.564 apathy:** refers to the Stoic ideal of dispassionateness. **l.595 frore:** cold, frosty. **l.596 Furies:** avenging goddesses. **l.632 Explores:** tests. **l.642 Ply stemming:** make headway against the wind. **l.647 impaled:** surrounded, fenced in. **l.652 Voluminous:** consisting of many coils. **l.654 cry:** pack. **l.662 night-hag:** Hecate, goddess of witchcraft. **l.665 labouring:** suffering eclipse. **l.677 admired:** wondered. **l.693 Conjured:** sworn together in a conspiracy. **l.815 lore:** lesson. **l.825 pretences:** assertions of claims. **l.829 unfounded:** bottomless. **l.842 buxom:** unresisting. **l.883 Erebus:** hell. **l.919 frith:** firth. **l.927 vans:** fans, i.e. wings. **l.933 pennons:** wings. **l.937 Instinct:** animated. **l.988 anarch:** Chaos. **l.989 incomposed:** wanting in composure. **l.1004 heaven:** the earth's sky (in l.1006, God's heaven). **l.1043 holds:** remains in. **l.1052 pendent world:** the created universe.

Samson Agonistes **l.11 day-spring:** dawn. **l.16 popular:** of the populace. **l.77 still:** invariably. **l.87 silent:** not shining. **l.89 vacant:** at leisure. **l.95 obvious:** exposed. **l.106 obnoxious:** exposed.

Everyman's Poetry

Titles available in this series all at £1.00

William Blake
ed. Peter Butter
0 460 87800 X

Robert Burns
ed. Donald Low
0 460 87814 X

Samuel Taylor Coleridge
ed. John Beer
0 460 87826 3

Thomas Gray
ed. Robert Mack
0 460 87805 0

Ivor Gurney
ed. George Walter
0 460 87797 6

George Herbert
ed. D. J. Enright
0 460 87795 X

Robert Herrick
ed. Douglas Brooks-Davies
0 460 87799 2

John Keats
ed. Nicholas Roe
0 460 87808 5

Henry Wadsworth Longfellow
ed. Anthony Thwaite
0 460 87821 2

John Milton
ed. Gordon Campbell
0 460 87813 1

Edgar Allan Poe
ed. Richard Gray
0 460 87804 2

Poetry Please!
Foreword by Charles
Causley
0 460 87824 7

Alexander Pope
ed. Douglas Brooks-Davies
0 460 87798 4

Lord Rochester
ed. Paddy Lyons
0 460 87819 0

Christina Rossetti
ed. Jan Marsh
0 460 87820 4

William Shakespeare
ed. Martin Dodsworth
0 460 87815 8

Alfred, Lord Tennyson
ed. Michael Baron
0 460 87802 6

R. S. Thomas
ed. Anthony Thwaite
0 460 87811 5

Walt Whitman
ed. Ellman Crasnow
0 460 87825 5

Oscar Wilde
ed. Robert Mighall
0 460 87803 4